soup

A Kosher Collection

Pam Reiss

M. EVANS AND COMPANY, INC.

New York

Edited by Marial Shea
Proofread by Lesley Cameron
Cover and interior design by Jacqui Thomas
Photography by Chris Freeland
Food Styling by Claire Stubbs
Ceramic bowls courtesy of The Gardiner Museum of Ceramic Art.

Printed and bound in Canada

LIBRARY OF CONGRESS CATALOGING IN PUBLICATION DATA

Reiss, Pamela.
Soup—a kosher collection / Pamela Reiss.
p. cm.
ISBN 1-59077-074-9 (pbk.)
1. Soups. 2. Cookery, Jewish. I. Title.
TX757.R55 2005
641.8'13—dc22
2004015625

Nutritional data is based on Imperial measurements. Information may vary if using metric measurements or altering quantities of ingredients.

Contents

❦ ACKNOWLEDGEMENTS

Thank you Mom and Dad for all of your support—in the book writing and in life. You have both passed on a love of good food, traditions I hope to always keep going and the ability to create the recipes to go along with the ideas. Thankfully you both love soup, and your tasting of each soup, again and again and again, was invaluable. Thanks to my sister Lisa for her ideas, taste buds, different viewpoint and support. Thanks to my legal team, Cary Reiss and Caroline Kiva; you both looked out for me, and your encouragement and English definitions of legalese helped tremendously. My thanks also go to all of my family and friends and everybody I've worked with throughout the years for countless ideas and encouragement.

Thanks to all the staff at Whitecap for guiding me through this process relatively unscathed and to Marial Shea for her spectacular editing. Thanks also to PJ Dempsey for her help in the early stages.

So many people, too many to list here, offered their encouragement, support, ideas and recipes when they found out about my soup project. I want to thank each and every one of you. Though not all of the soup ideas and recipes made it into the book, the excitement and interest everybody showed meant a great deal to me. Thank you.

Introduction

We all have strong food memories. From the potato pancakes your grandmother made at Chanukah, to the turkey and stuffing your great aunt prepared lovingly every year for Thanksgiving or the hotdogs from the baseball stadium, food plays a large part in our lives. We need it to survive. We use it to celebrate. We are comforted by it.

My food memories are almost all related to Jewish food. I remember my father's specialty, garlic brisket, served at my bat mitzvah over 15 years ago. I remember the chicken soup prepared by my baba (grandmother) and served at Friday night Sabbath dinner. My father doesn't do a bad job replicating her soup these days—but somehow she knew just how much fresh dill to add and his always seems to miss a little. Nobody could ever forget the hours spent preparing special foods for Passover and how wonderful it is every year to eat a piece of bread or a slice of pizza when the holiday is over. (Passover rules regarding ingredients and preparation are even stricter than rules for general kosher Jewish food.)

I also have memories of foods that are not considered typically Jewish. I remember the amazing feeling of accomplishment I felt when I first made pesto and bruschetta and my family loved it. I remember experimenting with my cousins to perfect our first sushi rolls and Thai and Chinese dishes.

My family has many food memories, both personal and professional. I grew up in Desserts Plus, my parents' kosher catering company. It seems my whole family has participated in the business: my sister, grandparents, aunts and uncles. Several cousins have put summers into the company during high school and university. I used to walk over after classes when I was in elementary school. Afternoons would be spent peeling potatoes or washing dishes. In high school, they expanded the business and opened a restaurant. After working in the restaurant during high school, I decided that I wanted to remain in the food industry. I went to the University of Minnesota and earned a degree in Hotel and Restaurant Management so I could join my parents in the family business.

In addition to my own bat mitzvah, I have memories of dozens of bar and bat mitzvahs we have catered for other families. And weddings. And baby namings. And circumcisions. And Chanukah parties. We helped create memories of life-cycle events in thousands of families' lives.

I am not a trained chef. Any cooking skills I have are either passed down by my family or self-taught. I will occasionally use cooking terms in a recipe, but I promise to include their definitions in the Definitions, Techniques and Ingredients section of the book or right in the recipe.

My theory of cooking is simple and straightforward. I have two rules: keep it simple and use the best ingredients. It amazes me when people say they can't cook. For those of you out there who feel this way, I hope this book helps. Just keep my two rules in mind at all times. I'm not saying that a complicated, time-consuming recipe can't be wonderful, but it's not a requirement for putting outstanding food on your dinner table. Simple, good, fresh ingredients and easy preparation—that's what it takes.

This book is designed to help you put the first course together. Soups, of course! Nothing beats a hot bowl of aromatic homemade soup on a cold winter day. It's a great starter to a meal. It can be elegant or rustic, simple or extravagant, a light beginning or a filling main course. Most often, it's even better reheated the day after you make it. In fact, most of these recipes can be frozen and later defrosted when you want a homemade treat. (I'll let you know when a recipe isn't meant to be frozen or reheated.) A simmering soup can fill a house with wonderful, inviting aromas. It can invoke memories of childhood dinners, surrounded by family, which none of us seem to have time for anymore.

I hope you use this book and make some wonderful soups. Who knows—maybe along with the soup, you'll be making some new cherished memories. Maybe after being snowed in one winter day, you'll pull out the book and make a big pot of Everything but the Kitchen Sink Soup and always remember that wonderful day when the whole family helped out and made a fantastic pot of soup together. Enjoy!

Definitions, Techniques and Ingredients

Kosher Food

What exactly is kosher food? There's a misconception that kosher food is food blessed by a rabbi. In fact, Kosher, or Kashrut, is a very specific set of rules concerning the preparation of food that goes back to biblical times and is still used by Jews around the world.

For example, kosher meat must be slaughtered in a specific way and processed properly, using salt to draw out excess blood from the animal. In most parts of the world, where there aren't large Jewish communities, only the front sections of ruminant animals with split hooves are used, because the back section of the animal is very difficult to process properly. Some examples of animals that are considered kosher and are readily available are cows and calves, sheep and lamb. No shellfish is allowed—only fish with scales and gills are kosher.

No meat products, meaning beef, veal, chicken, turkey, duck or lamb, can be eaten with any dairy products. The meat and the dairy can only be eaten on their own, and a person is to wait a specific amount of time between eating the two (time varies depending on where your family is from and how religious you are). Fish, fruit, vegetables and grains are considered parve, or neither meat nor milk, and may be eaten on their own or with either milk or meat.

❧ Techniques

Most of the recipes in this book, unless otherwise stated, use a basic soup technique. Generally, the soup is started by sautéing some vegetables and/or seasonings in olive oil or other fat for several minutes. A liquid along with vegetables, meat, beans and/or grains will be added to the pot. The pot will then be covered, the heat turned up to high and the soup brought to a boil. The heat will then be reduced, usually to low or medium. The soup is simmered gently, covered to keep the liquid from evaporating. (Occasionally, we want the liquid to evaporate to intensify flavors—but the directions will tell you if this is the case.) The soups will then vary—some will be ready to eat after simmering—others will need slurries or other things added to them.

DREDGING

Dredging something, usually in flour or breadcrumbs, simply means coating it. You dredge chicken in flour so that a nice, even layer of flour is left on the chicken.

JULIENNE

When you julienne food, usually a vegetable, it means that you cut it into long, thin strips.

PEELING TOMATOES

Peeling tomatoes is not a fun task, and I don't do it unless I have to. Why peel tomatoes? Because when you cook them, the flesh cooks down and leaves the skins intact. Nobody wants to eat tomato skins. If I'm cooking a chunky vegetable soup, or if I will be sending a puréed soup through a mesh strainer, I won't bother peeling tomatoes. If I want an elegant soup, or a soup with only a few ingredients, where the skins would be noticed, I'll take a little extra time and peel them. If you choose to peel tomatoes, start by boiling some water, enough to submerge them. Then, after washing the tomatoes, cut out the core and use a sharp paring knife to cut a little x into the very top of the tomato, just slicing through the skin. Have a bowl of ice water ready.

Submerge the tomatoes in the boiling water and simmer for one minute. Then, take them out and immediately plunge into the ice water. Once the tomatoes have cooled down, the peel should come right off. Riper tomatoes may need less time in the boiling water than less ripe ones.

PURÉEING SOUPS

Use a hand blender, blender or food processor to purée a soup. Do it in small batches and be very careful. Put a towel over the top of the food processor or blender to prevent any of the hot soup from spraying out. If you are concerned about processing the hot liquid, allow the soup to cool beforehand. You can then reheat the soup before serving (if it is a hot soup). I like to use a hand blender because of the ease factor—but using a blender will give you a smoother finished product.

ROASTING PEPPERS

You can buy these in a jar but they are usually packed in oil. I prefer to roast them myself, so that I can control the amount of oil in the recipe. They are also expensive, so if you're doing a Roasted Pepper Soup, it could end up costing you more than you'd like. If you are going to roast the peppers yourself, there are two ways to do it.

1. *In the oven.* Wash the peppers well. Place them on a cookie sheet or pan (I like to use parchment paper or aluminum foil to line the pan—it makes clean-up easier) and then into a preheated oven (400°F / 200°C). The peppers will need to be turned over a few times during roasting, first after ten minutes, and then a couple more times after five-minute intervals. You want the skin of the peppers to get nice and black. If this is happening a lot faster, turn them and then pull them out of the oven sooner. If it's taking longer, that's okay, just leave them in until they are ready. The peppers should take about 30 minutes—but watch them.

2. *On the grill (or gas element).* Place the well-washed peppers right on the grill or the gas stove element and keep turning them and moving them around until the skin is completely charred and black.

Once the skin is black, using either method, place the peppers in a bowl, cover with plastic wrap to seal the bowl and allow them to steam for about half an hour. When the peppers have cooled enough for you to handle, start peeling off the skin. Pull out the stem and all of the seeds. Don't run the peppers under water, because you'll rinse off a lot of the flavor.

SAUTÉING

When a recipe tells you to sauté something, it means to cook it in oil, stirring constantly. You want to keep the food moving in the pot or pan so nothing burns and everything is cooked evenly.

SLURRY

A slurry is a mixture made from a liquid and a starch. In most of my recipes, the slurry is milk whisked together with flour. Another common one is stock or water mixed with cornstarch. Generally slurries are used as a thickener for a soup or sauce.

SOUP POT

Unless otherwise stated, all soups are to be cooked in a good, heavy-bottomed soup pot. Obviously, some soups require a larger pot; the ingredients and serving amounts will give you an idea what size pot will be best. Almost every soup will need to be covered while simmering, so a lid is important, but aluminum foil could be substituted.

SWEATING ONIONS

This means to fry the onions in some fat until they just start to become tender. Generally, you do not do this over too high a heat—low to medium heat is best. You do not want to brown the onions when you are sweating them.

❧ Ingredients

LEEKS

These are dirty vegetables. They need to be well cleaned because mud gets packed in between the layers. In almost all cases, I just use the paler parts of the vegetable, close to the root. Discard the dark green parts, then cut about ¼ inch (5 mm) off the root end. Next, cut the leek in half, lengthwise. Separate the layers and allow to soak in cold water to break the mud up. Change the water at least once before the mud is all gone. Lift the leeks out of the water, so that whatever dirt is left remains at the bottom of the sink or bowl. After a final rinse, they are ready to slice up and use!

MILK / CREAM / NON-DAIRY CREAM SOUPS

Obviously, when you use milk or cream in a soup, it is dairy. To make a creamy, non-dairy soup, I substitute a non-dairy, liquid coffee whitener (Rich's) for the milk or cream. In addition to keeping the soup parve, it has the added benefit of not scorching easily.

OLIVE OIL

I almost always use olive oil—because I like it. Olive oil works well with both meat and dairy soups. I like the flavor and it's a good, healthy oil. I generally use a light olive oil, not an extra virgin, because there are usually so many other flavors going on in a soup that this more expensive, flavorful oil would be wasted. But there is no question that you can use whatever you like. Canola oil is fantastic. In the Asian-style soups, peanut oil would work well. For creamy and cheesy soups, you can use butter, but just be careful of its low burning point.

ONIONS

In recipes, I specify what kind of onion to use. In all honesty, the choice is not crucial—if you have a red onion, use it, or a yellow or a white onion. In fact, a shallot will usually fit the bill too. Generally, shallots and red onions are sweeter than yellow onions. If you want to maintain a certain color in your soup, that can affect your decision. But generally, peel any of the onions and they will work just fine. The only ones that can't be substituted are green. Although, to confuse matters even more, if a recipe calls for chives, then green onions (scallions) *are* a substitute you can use.

POTATOES

I usually use red potatoes in my soups. They hold their shape better and I prefer the texture. If I feel a soup needs a different potato, I'll specify which one to use. In almost all cases, I like the potatoes peeled. Again, if I want the skin on, I'll let you know. If the skin is left on, make sure to scrub the potato very well. Rinse peeled potatoes and keep them in a bowl of cold water while you are getting the rest of the ingredients together, so they don't oxidize and turn brown.

SALT AND PEPPER

The amount of seasoning you like in your soup is a completely subjective matter. Each recipe tells you how much salt and pepper I like, but you have to get to know your own tastes. My mother, for example, always adds salt to my soup and often tells me there is too much pepper in it for her taste. So hold back some salt and pepper and add it gradually, until you find the level you like. Just keep in mind a couple of facts: kosher meat has been salted during the koshering process. If you are not used to kosher meat, or if you don't use kosher meat in these recipes, the salt quantity will probably need to be adjusted. The other thing is that almost all foods, including desserts, need salt. If you taste something, and it seems to be lacking in flavor, the addition of salt will enhance the other flavors as well. Don't be afraid of salt—just don't overdo it!

STOCK

Many of the soups in this book call for stock. It's your choice—it can be chicken or vegetable stock. There are recipes for both in the book. I don't know about you, but I rarely have homemade stocks available. Although

they are my first choice, I often use a powdered, vegetarian chicken-flavored soup base when I make soup. This is a good option, because there are really good soup bases that are vegetarian, giving you the flexibility of using them in dairy soups. Use whatever is available that you like. It could be a good can of stock, a homemade version, or liquid or powdered bouillon. If you do use soup base, just follow the directions on the container for quantities, as different brands vary.

VEGETABLES AND FRUIT

Before using any fruits or vegetables, make sure to wash them well. There is a great debate about whether or not mushrooms should be washed. I always wash them. Just don't let them sit in a bowl of water or they will absorb too much—wash them briskly, but well, under running water. There may be pesticides, bugs and/or dirt on any produce you buy, so wash everything, including the skins of melons or other fruits and vegetables that you will discard.

WEIGHTS AND MEASURES

Using weights in a recipe is the most accurate way of measuring ingredients. If a recipe calls for one onion, the onion can range from 3 to 12 ounces. Most people don't have kitchen scales at home and aren't used to weighing every ingredient, so instead of weights for everything, I've included a chart with common vegetables and their approximate weights. When you're shopping for these ingredients, make use of the scales grocery stores supply in the produce section.

Keep in mind one important thing: while I have taken the time to perfect these recipes, you have room to play. Soups are very forgiving and if a recipe calls for a small carrot, or 2 ounces of rice, if you use a medium carrot or 3 ounces of rice, it will still work (you might need to add some extra stock, but it will work).

Here are some approximate weights:

	SMALL	MEDIUM	LARGE
BEET	4 oz. | 125 g	8 oz. | 250 g	10 oz. | 300 g
BUTTERNUT SQUASH	10 oz. | 300 g	14 oz. | 425 g	20 oz. | 600 g
CARROT	2–3 oz. | 50–75 g	4 oz. | 125 g	6 oz. | 175 g
CELERY—1 stalk	–	2 oz. | 50 g	–
CUCUMBER	8 oz. | 250 g	10 oz. | 300 g	12 oz. | 375 g
LEEK	2 oz. | 50 g	3 oz. | 75 g	4 oz. | 125 g
ONION—yellow, red, white	4–6 oz. | 125–175 g	8 oz. | 250 g	10 oz. | 300 g
RED/GREEN PEPPER	4 oz. | 125 g	6 oz. | 175 g	12 oz. | 375 g
RED POTATO	4–6 oz. | 125–175 g	8 oz. | 250 g	10 oz. | 300 g
ROMA (ITALIAN PLUM) TOMATO	–	3 oz. | 75 g	–
SHALLOT	1 oz. | 25 g	2 oz. | 50 g	3 oz. | 75 g
SWEET POTATO	8 oz. | 250 g	12–14 oz. | 375–425 g	16–18 oz. | 500–550 g
TURNIP	2 oz. | 50 g	3 oz. | 75 g	4 oz. | 125 g
ZUCCHINI	4 oz. | 125 g	6 oz. | 175 g	8 oz. | 250 g

Here are some approximate volumes:

	1 OZ.	¼ LB.	½ LB.	1 LB.
GRATED CHEESE	¼ cup | 50 mL	1 cup | 250 mL	2 cups | 500 mL	4 cups | 1 L
MUSHROOMS	⅓ cup | 75 mL	1½ cups | 375 mL	3 cups | 750 mL	6 cups | 1.5 L

Parve • Vegetarian Soups

Vegetable Stock

2 large carrots, peeled and cut into 2-inch (5-cm) pieces

2 medium yellow onions, peeled and quartered

6–7 stalks celery, cut into 2-inch (5-cm) pieces

2 medium leeks, white part only, cut in half lengthwise

1 small parsnip, peeled and cut into 2-inch (5-cm) pieces

1 tsp. | 5 mL whole peppercorns

2 tsp. | 10 mL salt

12 cups | 3 L cold water

4 cups | 1 L fresh Italian parsley (8 oz. | 250 g), stalks and leaves

Once this stock is made, it's great as a base for other soups. Another option is to strain the stock, add some julienned carrot, celery and zucchini and simmer just until tender, then serve.

METHOD

Place all the ingredients into a pot and bring to a boil over high heat. Reduce heat to medium-low and simmer for 15 minutes uncovered, then add a lid and simmer another 25 minutes.

Strain out all of the vegetables, and use the clear stock as a base for vegetarian soup.

PER SERVING

65	Calories
trace Fat	(6.1% calories from fat)
2 g	Protein
15 g	Carbohydrate
4 g	Dietary Fiber
0 mg	Cholesterol
615 mg	Sodium

SERVES 8 | PARVE • FREEZES • PASSOVER

Everything but the Kitchen Sink Soup

1 small yellow onion, peeled and shredded

2 small carrots, peeled and shredded

1 stalk celery, finely chopped

1 medium zucchini, shredded

¼ lb. | 125 g button mushrooms, shredded

1 small red potato, peeled and shredded

1 medium leek, white part, finely sliced

1 medium parsnip, peeled and shredded

small piece of butternut squash (¼ lb. | 125 g), peeled and shredded

⅓ cup | 75 mL pearl barley, rinsed and drained

⅓ cup | 75 mL red lentils, rinsed and drained

4–6 cloves garlic (1 Tbsp. | 15 mL), crushed

9 cups | 2.25 L stock

2½ tsp. | 12 mL salt

½ tsp. | 2 mL black pepper

1 small, red bell pepper, finely diced

⅓ cup | 75 mL white rice

¾ cup | 175 mL frozen corn kernels

This soup started off as a way to use up a bunch of bits and pieces in my kitchen. It's now my mother's favorite soup. Shredding most of the vegetables gives it a unique texture. Feel free to add or subtract ingredients.

METHOD

Place everything but the red bell pepper, rice and corn into a pot. Cover and bring the mixture to a gentle simmer and cook for half an hour.

Add the pepper, rice and corn and simmer for another 15 minutes, or until the rice is tender.

PER SERVING

110	Calories
1 g	Fat (9.2% calories from fat)
4 g	Protein
22 g	Carbohydrate
3 g	Dietary Fiber
0 mg	Cholesterol
1571 mg	Sodium

SERVES 12 | PARVE · FREEZES

Hearty Fall Vegetable Soup

1 small yellow onion, peeled and coarsely chopped

2 Tbsp. | 25 mL olive oil

1 stalk celery, coarsely chopped

1 small carrot, peeled and sliced ¼ inch (5 mm) thick

2 small red potatoes, peeled and cut into
½-inch (1-cm) cubes

4–6 cloves garlic (1 Tbsp. | 15 mL), crushed

3 Tbsp. | 45 mL paprika

1 tsp. | 5 mL salt

¼ tsp. | 1 mL black pepper

2 bay leaves

1 Tbsp. | 15 mL granulated sugar

1 cup | 250 mL red wine

1 can (5½ oz. | 156 mL) tomato paste

1 can (28 oz. | 796 mL) diced tomatoes

5 cups | 1.25 L water

¼ lb. | 125 g button mushrooms, quartered

1 small zucchini, cut into ½-inch | 1-cm cubes

1½ cups | 375 mL frozen green beans

1⅓ cups | 325 mL frozen corn kernels

A perfect autumn soup. Use whatever red wine you like to drink—you can leave it out, but it adds a nice acidity, and the alcohol will cook off.

METHOD

In a soup pot, over medium heat, sauté the onion in olive oil, 2–3 minutes.

Add the celery, carrot, potatoes, seasonings and granulated sugar. Sauté 1–2 minutes.

Add the red wine and cook 3–4 minutes, giving the alcohol a chance to cook off.

Add the tomato paste, diced tomatoes, water and mushrooms and cover. Turn heat to high and bring to a boil, then reduce heat to medium-low and simmer 25 minutes.

Add the zucchini, green beans and corn and allow to simmer 10 minutes.

Pull out the bay leaves and serve.

PER SERVING

145	Calories
3 g	Fat (21.7% calories from fat)
4 g	Protein
24 g	Carbohydrate
4 g	Dietary Fiber
0 mg	Cholesterol
485 mg	Sodium

SERVES 10 | PARVE · FREEZES

Roasted Vegetable Soup

½ lb. | 250 g mushrooms, washed and quartered

2 medium bell peppers, washed, seeded and cut into
¾-inch | 2-cm cubes

1 medium zucchini, washed and sliced ½ inch | 1 cm thick

1 small eggplant (about 10 oz. | 300 g), washed and cut
into ¾-inch | 2-cm cubes

4 stalks celery, washed and sliced ½ inch | 1 cm thick

1 medium carrot, washed, peeled and sliced
¼ inch | 5 mm thick

6–7 medium Roma (Italian Plum) tomatoes
(1¼ lbs. | 625 g), peeled and coarsely chopped

¼ cup | 50 mL olive oil

1½ tsp. | 7 mL dried oregano

1½ tsp. | 7 mL dried basil

1½ tsp. | 7 mL salt

½ tsp. | 2 mL black pepper

4–6 cloves garlic (1 Tbsp. | 15 mL), crushed

1 can (28 oz. | 796 mL) diced tomatoes

4 cups | 1 L water

This is one of only a few soups I do not recommend freezing. It would still taste great but there would be no texture at all because the vegetables get too mushy and disintegrate.

METHOD

Preheat oven to 400°F (200°C). In a deep, ovenproof dish, place all of the vegetables, olive oil, oregano, basil, salt and pepper. Toss everything together and roast for 45 minutes, stirring the mixture after 20 minutes.

Add the crushed garlic, canned tomatoes and water. Mix well and cover with aluminum foil. Place back in the oven and roast for another 45 minutes.

Check for seasoning and serve!

PER SERVING

106	Calories
6 g Fat	(45.8% calories from fat)
3 g	Protein
13 g	Carbohydrate
4 g	Dietary Fiber
0 mg	Cholesterol
470 mg	Sodium

SERVES 10 | DAIRY • DON'T FREEZE

Vegetable Barley Soup

½ small yellow onion, peeled and finely chopped

1 small carrot, peeled, halved lengthwise then cut into ¼-inch | 5-mm half-circles

1 stalk celery, thinly sliced

6 oz. | 175 g button mushrooms, cut into ¼-inch | 5-mm slices

½ small turnip, peeled and diced small

1 bay leaf

⅓ cups | 75 mL pearl barley, rinsed well

7 cups | 1.75 L stock

1 tsp. | 5 mL salt

¼ tsp. | 1 mL black pepper

¾ cup | 175 mL green beans, cut into 1-inch | 2.5-cm pieces

Add any vegetables you like. A great soup for using up vegetables from your garden. Make big batches in the late summer and freeze—perfect for a chilly fall dinner.

METHOD

Place everything but green beans into a soup pot. Cover and bring to a boil over high heat. Reduce heat and simmer gently for 20 minutes on medium-low.

Add green beans and continue to simmer for 10–15 minutes, or until the barley is tender.

Remove the bay leaf and serve.

PER SERVING

101	Calories
2 g	Fat (13.7% calories from fat)
4 g	Protein
18 g	Carbohydrate
4 g	Dietary Fiber
0 mg	Cholesterol
2109 mg	Sodium

SERVES 6 | PARVE · FREEZES

Winter Vegetable Soup

1 small yellow onion, peeled and chopped small

2 Tbsp. | 25 mL olive oil

2 cloves garlic (1 tsp. | 5 mL), crushed

1 tsp. | 5 mL salt

¼ tsp. | 1 mL black pepper

1 bay leaf

¼ tsp. | 1 mL nutmeg

¼ tsp. | 1 mL coriander

¼ tsp. | 1 mL cumin

¼ tsp. | 1 mL ginger

¼ tsp. | 1 mL chili powder

¼ tsp. | 1 mL paprika

1 medium carrot, peeled and cut into ½-inch | 1-cm dice

1 small rutabaga, peeled and cut into ½-inch | 1-cm dice

1 small sweet potato, peeled and cut into
½-inch | 1-cm dice

1 medium red potato, peeled and cut into
½-inch | 1-cm dice

10 cups | 2.5 L stock

4 cups | 1 L firmly packed spinach leaves (½ lb. | 250 g),
sliced into strips

1 can (16 oz. or 19 oz. | 540 mL) chickpeas, rinsed
and drained

*A ton of flavor and amazing aromas. The spinach adds
freshness to an otherwise wintry soup.*

METHOD

Over medium heat, sauté onion in olive oil for 4–5 minutes.

Add all of the seasonings and spices and sauté another
minute, stirring constantly.

Add all of the vegetables, except the spinach, and sauté
another minute.

Add stock, cover and bring to a boil. Reduce heat to
medium-low and simmer 30 minutes.

Add spinach and chickpeas and cook for 1–2 minutes.

Remove bay leaf, check for seasoning and serve!

PER SERVING	
169	Calories
5 g	Fat (24.4% calories from fat)
6 g	Protein
27 g	Carbohydrate
5 g	Dietary Fiber
0 mg	Cholesterol
1888 mg	Sodium

SERVES 10 | DAIRY • FREEZES

Root Soup

1 medium beet, peeled and cut into ½-inch | 1-cm cubes

1 medium carrot, peeled and cut into ½-inch | 1-cm cubes

2 small red potatoes, peeled and cut into ½-inch | 1-cm cubes

1 large turnip, peeled and cut into ½-inch | 1-cm cubes

1 small sweet potato, peeled and cut into ½-inch | 1-cm cubes

1 small yellow onion, peeled and coarsely chopped

1 stalk celery (2 oz. | 50 g), thinly sliced

1 can (16 oz. or 19 oz. | 540 mL) diced tomatoes

7 cups | 1.75 L water

1 cup | 250 mL red wine

1 tsp. | 5 mL salt

¼ tsp. | 1 mL black pepper

2 bay leaves

3 Tbsp. | 45 mL granulated sugar

This soup uses some of the great vegetables available during the winter. It's a variation on borscht and would be delicious topped with sour cream.

METHOD

Place ingredients in a soup pot, cover and bring to a boil over high heat. Reduce heat to medium-low and simmer for about 1 hour. The soup is done when the harder vegetables, like the beets and carrots, are fork-tender. Remove the bay leaves before serving.

PER SERVING

100	Calories
trace Fat	(2.2% calories from fat)
2 g	Protein
20 g	Carbohydrate
3 g	Dietary Fiber
0 mg	Cholesterol
343 mg	Sodium

SERVES 10 | PARVE WITHOUT SOUR CREAM •
FREEZES • PASSOVER

Sweet Potato and Apple Soup

½ small red onion, peeled and coarsely chopped

2 Tbsp. | 25 mL olive oil

1 tsp. | 5 mL fresh ginger, minced very fine

¼ tsp. | 1 mL ground cinnamon

⅛ tsp. | .5 mL ground nutmeg

1 tsp. | 5 mL salt

¼ tsp. | 1 mL black pepper

2–3 large Golden Delicious apples (1 lb. | 500 g), peeled, cored and coarsely cubed

2 small sweet potatoes (1 lb. | 500 g), peeled and coarsely cubed

6 cups | 1.5 L stock

Both apples and sweet potatoes go well with nutmeg, ginger and cinnamon, so why not try them together with these flavors. Add some cream as a garnish.

METHOD

Sauté onion in olive oil over medium-low heat for 5–8 minutes, until tender and just starting to brown.

Add all of the spices and sauté another 30 seconds, stirring constantly.

Add the apples, sweet potato and stock, cover and bring to a boil on high heat. Reduce heat and simmer gently on medium-low for 12–15 minutes, until the sweet potato and apples are fork-tender.

Purée the soup. See *Puréeing Soups* on page 9 in the Techniques section.

PER SERVING

155	Calories
6 g	Fat (33.8% calories from fat)
3 g	Protein
24 g	Carbohydrate
3 g	Dietary Fiber
0 mg	Cholesterol
1849 mg	Sodium

SERVES 6 | PARVE WITHOUT CREAM · FREEZES · PASSOVER

Roasted Garlic and Potato Soup

1 whole garlic bulb, roasted and peeled

1 small yellow onion, peeled and coarsely chopped

2 Tbsp. | 25 mL olive oil

4–5 medium red potatoes (1½ lbs. | 750 g), peeled and cut into ½-inch | 1-cm cubes

1 tsp. | 5 mL salt

¼ tsp. | 1 mL black pepper

2 large fresh sage leaves, sliced into ¼-inch | 5-mm strips (or ¼ tsp. | 1 mL dried)

4 cups | 1 L stock

Roasting the garlic takes away the sharpness found in raw garlic and gives the soup a subtle, sweeter garlic flavor. If you are a true garlic lover, try adding more roasted garlic.

METHOD

Preheat oven to 350°F (180°C). Wrap the garlic bulb in aluminum foil, place in the oven and roast for approximately 45 minutes. Allow to cool, then peel.

Over medium-low heat, sauté the onion in olive oil for 5–8 minutes, until wilted, but not browned.

Add the potatoes, garlic, salt, pepper, sage leaves and stock. Cover soup pot and turn heat up to high. When the soup reaches a boil, reduce the heat and simmer gently for 15–20 minutes on medium-low, or until the potatoes are fork-tender.

Purée the soup. See *Puréeing Soups* on page 9 in the Techniques section.

PER SERVING

161	Calories
5 g	Fat (29.5% calories from fat)
4 g	Protein
25 g	Carbohydrate
2 g	Dietary Fiber
0 mg	Cholesterol
1353 mg	Sodium

SERVES 6 | PARVE · FREEZES · PASSOVER

Potato Cabbage Soup

1 small yellow onion, peeled and finely chopped

2 Tbsp. | 25 mL olive oil

2 tsp. | 10 mL whole caraway seeds

1 tsp. | 5 mL salt

½ tsp. | 2 mL black pepper

4 cups | 1 L cabbage (¾ lb. | 375 g), finely shredded

4 medium red potatoes (1½ lbs. | 750 g), peeled and cut into ⅓-inch | 8-mm cubes

6 cups | 1.5 L stock

The caraway seeds work well with the potatoes and cabbage. This is a soup that makes the Eastern European part of me very happy.

METHOD

Over medium-low heat, sauté the onion in olive oil for 5–7 minutes.

Add caraway seeds, salt and pepper and sauté another minute.

Add the cabbage and cook for 2–3 minutes, until it starts to wilt.

Add potatoes and stock, cover and bring to a boil. Reduce heat and simmer 20 minutes on medium-low, or until the potatoes are tender.

PER SERVING

175	Calories
6 g Fat	(29.8% calories from fat)
5 g	Protein
27 g	Carbohydrate
4 g	Dietary Fiber
0 mg	Cholesterol
1857 mg	Sodium

SERVES 6 | PARVE • FREEZES • PASSOVER

French Onion Soup

4 medium yellow onions (2 lbs. | 1 kg), peeled, halved and sliced into ¼-inch | 5-mm rings

2 Tbsp. | 25 mL olive oil

2 tsp. | 10 mL granulated sugar

⅓ cup | 75 mL dry red wine

6 cups | 1.5 L stock

1 bay leaf

½ tsp. | 2 mL black pepper

1 tsp. | 5 mL salt

3 tsp. | 15 mL soy sauce

I love onion soup. Have it on its own, toss in some croutons and Parmesan cheese, or float a slice of French bread in it, top with a slice of Swiss cheese and broil until the cheese is nice and gooey. My favorite comfort food.

METHOD

Place onions, olive oil and granulated sugar in a heavy soup pot and stir well to coat. Cover the pot and cook for 15 minutes on medium-high, stirring frequently.

Take the lid off the pot, turn the heat up to high and cook another 15 minutes, stirring frequently. The onions will soften and get a lot of brown color on them. This is what you want—brown but not burned.

Add the wine and simmer 2–3 minutes, scraping all the good stuff from the bottom of the pot and allowing the wine to reduce.

Add stock, bay leaf, black pepper, salt and soy sauce. Cover and bring to a boil. Reduce heat and allow to simmer for 40 minutes on low.

PER SERVING

130	Calories
6 g	Fat (41.7% calories from fat
3 g	Protein
15 g	Carbohydrate
3 g	Dietary Fiber
0 mg	Cholesterol
2023 mg	Sodium

SERVES 6 | PARVE WITHOUT CHEESE • FREEZES

Curried Potato Soup

1 small yellow onion, peeled and coarsely chopped

¼ cup | 50 mL olive oil

1–2 cloves garlic (1 tsp. | 5 mL), crushed

1 small jalapeno, seeded and diced fine

1⅓ Tbsp. | 20 mL curry powder

½ tsp. | 2 mL cumin powder

¼ tsp. | 1 mL ground coriander

⅛ tsp. | .5 mL ground ginger

1 tsp. | 5 mL salt

⅛ tsp. | .5 mL ground nutmeg

⅛ tsp. | .5 mL ground cardamom

¼ tsp. | 1 mL ground turmeric

½ tsp. | 2 mL dry mustard

2 small sweet potatoes (1 lb. | 500 g), peeled and cut into ½-inch | 1-cm cubes

2–3 medium red potatoes (1 lb. | 500 g), peeled and cut into ½-inch | 1-cm cubes

7 cups | 1.75 L stock

1 cup | 250 mL frozen green peas

1 Tbsp. | 15 mL lemon juice

This is samosa filling in soup form. It's a little spicy, and full of flavor and amazing aromas. Throw in some rinsed canned chickpeas for a complete meal.

METHOD

Over medium heat, sauté the onion in olive oil for 3–4 minutes.

Add the garlic, jalapeno and all of the seasonings. Sauté 1–2 minutes, stirring constantly, until the spices start to release their aromas.

Add the sweet and red potatoes and sauté 1–2 minutes.

Add the stock, cover and bring to a boil. Reduce the heat and gently simmer for 30 minutes, until potatoes are fork-tender.

Using a potato masher, mash about half of the potatoes. This will thicken the soup.

Add the peas and lemon juice and cook 2–3 minutes.

PER SERVING

194	Calories
8 g	Fat (37.3% calories from fat)
4 g	Protein
27 g	Carbohydrate
4 g	Dietary Fiber
0 mg	Cholesterol
1595 mg	Sodium

SERVES 8 | PARVE • FREEZES

Carrot Dill Soup

1 medium yellow onion, peeled and finely chopped

2 Tbsp. | 25 mL olive oil

5–6 medium carrots (1½ lbs. | 750 g), peeled and thinly sliced

1½ tsp. | 7 mL salt

¼ tsp. | 1 mL black pepper

5 cups | 1.25 L stock

3 Tbsp. | 45 mL fresh dill, finely chopped

Carrots and dill are natural partners. Although there are no dairy products in the recipe, the soup has an almost buttery flavor.

METHOD

Over medium-low heat, sweat the onion in olive oil for 5–7 minutes, until wilted, but not browned.

Add carrots, salt, pepper and stock. Cover, bring to a boil and simmer over low heat for 20 minutes, or until the carrots are tender.

Purée the soup. See *Puréeing Soups* on page 9 in the Techniques sections.

Add the fresh dill and heat 1–2 minutes.

PER SERVING

172	Calories
8 g	Fat (42.8% calories from fat)
4 g	Protein
22 g	Carbohydrate
6 g	Dietary Fiber
0 mg	Cholesterol
2709 mg	Sodium

SERVES 4 | PARVE • FREEZES • PASSOVER

Beet Borscht

10–12 small beets (2 lbs. | 1 kg), peeled and cut into ½-inch | 1-cm cubes

1 small carrot, peeled and thinly sliced

1 small yellow onion, peeled and coarsely chopped

3 stalks celery, chopped into ½-inch | 1-cm cubes

1 can (28 oz. | 796 mL) crushed tomatoes

8 cups | 2 L cold water

1 Tbsp. | 15 mL salt

⅛ tsp. | .5 mL black pepper

1 Tbsp. | 15 mL granulated sugar

1½ Tbsp. | 20 mL lemon juice

This is one of those soups my Russian ancestry makes me crave occasionally. My mother likes it a little sweeter, my father likes it served with sour cream, my sister likes it with potatoes—but I like it like this!

Another version, which I love, is meat borscht. Start by bringing some stewing beef up to a low boil in the 8 cups (2 L) of water, skimming off any residue and simmering for approximately half an hour—until the meat is cooked and tender. Then add the vegetables and follow the recipe. The meat will be left sweet and tender.

METHOD

Place the beets, carrot, onion, celery, tomatoes and water in a soup pot. Cover and bring to a boil over high heat. Reduce the heat to medium, and simmer for 45 minutes, or until the beets are fork-tender.

Add the salt, pepper, granulated sugar and lemon juice. The seasoning may need adjusting, but it should have a subtle sweet-and-sour flavor.

PER SERVING

58	Calories
trace Fat	(3.6% calories from fat)
2 g	Protein
13 g	Carbohydrate
3 g	Dietary Fiber
0 mg	Cholesterol
826 mg	Sodium

SERVES 10 | PARVE • FREEZES • PASSOVER

Fresh Asparagus Soup

1½ lbs. | 750 g asparagus

1 small yellow onion, peeled and finely chopped

2 Tbsp. | 25 mL olive oil

3 cups | 750 mL stock

⅛ tsp. | .5 mL black pepper

½ tsp. | 2 mL salt

If you love asparagus, try this soup. Its simple ingredients showcase the asparagus.

METHOD

Prepare the asparagus. If the stalks are large, use a vegetable peeler to peel them from just below the tips all the way to the end. Trim off the very end. Cut the asparagus into 1-inch (2.5-cm) pieces. If the stalks are very young and thin, trim off the very end and cut into 1-inch (2.5-cm) pieces.

Over medium-low heat sauté the onion in olive oil for 5–8 minutes.

Add stock, pepper, salt and asparagus stems (reserving tips), cover, turn heat to high and bring to a boil. Reduce heat and simmer for 10 minutes.

Purée the soup. See *Puréeing Soups* on page 9 in the Techniques sections.

Bring soup back to a simmer and add asparagus tips. Simmer for another 8–10 minutes, until asparagus is tender, but not overcooked.

PER SERVING

107	Calories
8 g	Fat (62.0% calories from fat)
3 g	Protein
7 g	Carbohydrate
2 g	Dietary Fiber
0 mg	Cholesterol
1382 mg	Sodium

SERVES 4 | PARVE · DON'T FREEZE · PASSOVER

Asparagus and Corn Eggdrop Soup

1¼ lbs. | 625 g fresh asparagus

1 small yellow onion, peeled and finely chopped

2 Tbsp. | 25 mL olive oil

6 cups | 1.5 L stock

1½ tsp. | 7 mL salt

½ tsp. | 2 mL black pepper

1½ cups | 375 mL frozen corn kernels

2 Tbsp. | 25 mL cornstarch

½ cup | 125 mL cold water

2 eggs

2 tsp. | 10 mL sesame oil

Asparagus and corn are a great combination. The sesame oil and eggs give this soup a silky texture with an Asian twist.

METHOD

Prepare the asparagus. If the stalks are large, use a vegetable peeler to peel them from just below the tips all the way to the end. Trim off the very end. Cut the asparagus into 1-inch (2.5-cm) pieces. If the stalks are very young and thin, trim off the very end and cut into 1-inch (2.5-cm) pieces.

Over medium-low heat, sauté the onion in olive oil for 5–8 minutes, until softened.

Add the stock, cover and bring to a boil over high heat. Reduce heat and allow the soup to simmer gently for 8–10 minutes.

Add the asparagus, salt, pepper and corn and simmer for 7–9 minutes, until the asparagus is just underdone.

In a separate bowl, whisk together the cornstarch and cold water. Add this mixture to the soup and allow to simmer another 2–3 minutes, until the soup has thickened.

In another bowl, whisk together the eggs and the sesame oil. In a slow, thin stream, pour this mixture into the soup. Wait 10 seconds then stir the soup to break up the long streams of cooked egg.

PER SERVING

159	Calories
9 g	Fat (48.1% calories from fat)
7 g	Protein
15 g	Carbohydrate
3 g	Dietary Fiber
62 mg	Cholesterol
2039 mg	Sodium

SERVES 6 | PARVE • DON'T FREEZE

Apple and Fennel Soup

2–3 shallots, peeled and finely chopped

2 Tbsp. | 25 mL olive oil

1 small fennel bulb (¾ lb. | 375 g), cleaned and thinly sliced

4–5 large Golden Delicious apples (1½ lbs. | 750 g), peeled, cored and coarsely chopped

1 bay leaf

1½ tsp. | 7 mL salt

¼ tsp. | 1 mL pepper

6 cups | 1.5 L stock

A light soup with tart apple and warm liquorice flavors.

METHOD

Over medium heat, sauté shallots in olive oil for 4–5 minutes, stirring frequently.

Add fennel, apples and seasonings. Keep stirring and sautéing until the apples begin to break down, about 5 minutes.

Add stock, cover and bring to a boil over high heat. Reduce the temperature and simmer until the vegetables and apple are tender, about 20 minutes.

Remove bay leaf. Purée the soup (see *Puréeing Soups* on page 9 in the Techniques section) and serve.

PER SERVING

100	Calories
4 g	Fat (38.1% calories from fat)
2 g	Protein
14 g	Carbohydrate
2 g	Dietary Fiber
0 mg	Cholesterol
1533 mg	Sodium

SERVES 8 | PARVE • FREEZES • PASSOVER

Jade Soup

1 medium leek, cut in half lengthwise and sliced into
¼-inch | 5-mm half-circles, white part only

2 Tbsp. | 25 mL olive oil

4–6 cloves garlic (1 Tbsp. | 15 mL), crushed

4 cups | 1 L stock

1 medium red potato, peeled and cubed

1½ tsp. | 7 mL salt

½ tsp. | 2 mL black pepper

1 medium zucchini, cut in half lengthwise and sliced
into ½-inch | 1-cm half-circles

2 cups | 500 mL firmly packed spinach leaves
(¼ lb. | 125 g)

1 cup | 250 mL arugula (firmly packed)

¼ cup | 50 mL fresh parsley

¼ cup | 50 mL fresh chives

¼ cup | 50 mL fresh basil (firmly packed)

*This soup gets its name from its beautiful green color.
In addition to the punch of color, it also has a punch of
flavor. In the winter, cut back the portion and eat it hot
as a starter; during the summer chill it and serve for a
light dinner on a hot night.*

METHOD

Over medium-low heat, sauté the leek in olive oil for
4–5 minutes, until wilted.

Add the garlic and sauté another minute, stirring constantly.

Add the stock, potato, salt and pepper, cover and bring to
a boil over high heat. Turn the heat down and simmer on
low for 10 minutes.

Add the zucchini and simmer another 10 minutes.

Add the spinach, arugula and herbs and simmer another
2–3 minutes.

Purée the soup. See *Puréeing Soups* on page 9 in the
Techniques section.

PER SERVING

150	Calories
8 g	Fat (47.0% calories from fat)
4 g	Protein
16 g	Carbohydrate
3 g	Dietary Fiber
0 mg	Cholesterol
2305 mg	Sodium

SERVES 4 | PARVE • FREEZES • PASSOVER

Red Cabbage and Apple Soup

1 lb. | 500 g red cabbage, finely shredded

8 cups | 2 L stock

3 large Golden Delicious apples (1 lb. | 500 g), peeled, cored and shredded

2 bay leaves

1½ tsp. | 7 mL salt

½ tsp. | 2 mL black pepper

1 small yellow onion, peeled and finely chopped

½ tsp. | 2 mL caraway seeds

A twist on cabbage borscht. The color is shockingly pink and the Granny Smith apples add the tartness that usually comes from sour salt.

METHOD

Place all ingredients in a soup pot, cover and bring to a boil over high heat. Reduce heat and simmer for 50 minutes on medium-low.

PER SERVING

87	Calories
2 g	Fat (17.9% calories from fat)
3 g	Protein
16 g	Carbohydrate
3 g	Dietary Fiber
0 mg	Cholesterol
2523 mg	Sodium

SERVES 6 | PARVE · FREEZES

Beet Borscht | *page 27*

Hot and Sour Soup | *page 61*

Baked Potato Soup | *page 74*

Roasted Bell Pepper Soup | *page 85*

Cabbage Soup

1 medium yellow onion, peeled and finely chopped

1 small carrot, peeled and thinly sliced

2 stalks celery, thinly sliced

1½ lbs. | 750 g green cabbage, cut into 1-inch- | 2.5-cm square pieces

2 small red potatoes, peeled and cut into ½-inch | 1-cm cubes

1 can (28 oz. | 796 mL) diced tomatoes

8 cups | 2 L water

2 tsp. | 10 mL salt

½ tsp. | 2 mL black pepper

1½ Tbsp. | 20 mL paprika

8–12 cloves garlic (2 Tbsp. | 25 mL), crushed

2 bay leaves

This is a chop, dump and cook soup—a hearty vegetable stew that's filling and easy to make.

METHOD

Chop all the vegetables and put them with the other ingredients in a soup pot. Cover and bring to a boil. Simmer over medium-low heat for approximately 1 hour, until all the vegetables are tender.

Remove bay leaves and serve.

PER SERVING	
51	Calories
trace	Fat (5.1% calories from fat)
2 g	Protein
12 g	Carbohydrate
2 g	Dietary Fiber
0 mg	Cholesterol
564 mg	Sodium

SERVES 10 | PARVE • FREEZES • PASSOVER

Zucchini Soup

1 small yellow onion, peeled and coarsely chopped

2 Tbsp. | 25 mL olive oil

1–2 cloves garlic (1 tsp. | 5 mL), crushed

1 large red potato, peeled and sliced ¼ inch | 5 mm thick

4–5 medium zucchini (2 lbs. | 1 kg), sliced ½ inch | 1 cm thick

2 tsp. | 10 mL salt

¼ tsp. | 1 mL black pepper

5 cups | 1.25 L stock

I love zucchini when it's cooked well. This soup is pure zucchini, with nothing else to overpower the flavor. It's important to slice the potatoes relatively thin, about half the thickness of the zucchini, so the zucchini doesn't overcook waiting for the potatoes.

METHOD

Sauté onion in olive oil over medium-low heat for 5–8 minutes, until wilted, but not browned.

Add garlic and sauté 30 seconds, stirring constantly.

Add potato, zucchini, salt, pepper and stock. Cover and bring to a boil. Reduce heat and simmer for 5–8 minutes on medium-low, until the potato and zucchini are fork-tender.

Purée the soup. See *Puréeing Soups* on page 9 in the Techniques section.

PER SERVING

130	Calories
6 g	Fat (37.4% calories from fat)
4 g	Protein
17 g	Carbohydrate
3 g	Dietary Fiber
0 mg	Cholesterol
1955 mg	Sodium

SERVES 6 | PARVE · FREEZES · PASSOVER

❧ Spicy Zucchini Soup

1 small yellow onion, peeled and finely chopped

1 whole red chili pepper, cored, seeded and finely minced

2 Tbsp. | 25 mL olive oil

2 medium zucchini (1 lb. | 500 g), grated

4–6 cloves garlic (1 Tbsp. | 15 mL), crushed

1 tsp. | 5 mL salt

¼ tsp. | 1 mL black pepper

5 cups | 1.25 L stock

2 tsp. | 10 mL sambal oelek (chili sauce)

1 Tbsp. | 15 mL fresh lime juice

I use the small, red Thai chilies for this soup, but if you are a spice lover, experiment with different peppers, like the habanero. If you're not sure about spices, go easy and reduce the sambal oelek to ½ tsp. (2 mL) to start and work your way up!

METHOD

Over medium-low heat sauté onion and chili pepper in olive oil for 5–7 minutes, until wilted.

Add the zucchini, garlic, salt and pepper and sauté until the zucchini starts to release its juices, 2–3 minutes.

Add the stock and sambal oelek, cover, turn heat up to high and bring to a boil. Reduce heat to medium-low and simmer for 8–10 minutes.

Add lime juice and serve.

PER SERVING

82	Calories
6 g	Fat (58.3% calories from fat)
2 g	Protein
6 g	Carbohydrate
1 g	Dietary Fiber
0 mg	Cholesterol
1596 mg	Sodium

SERVES 6 | PARVE · FREEZES · PASSOVER

Spinach Coconut Curry Soup

2–3 medium shallots (¼ lb. | 125 g), peeled and finely chopped

3 Tbsp. | 45 mL olive oil

1½ Tbsp. | 22 mL medium curry powder

¼ tsp. | 1 mL ground coriander

¼ tsp. | 1 mL ground cumin

½ tsp. | 2 mL dry mustard

1 tsp. | 5 mL salt

¼ tsp. | 1 mL ground nutmeg

¼ tsp. | 1 mL ground ginger

½ tsp. | 2 mL ground turmeric

¼ tsp. | 1 mL ground cardamom

1–2 cloves garlic (1 tsp. | 5 mL), ground

8 cups | 2 L firmly packed spinach leaves (1 lb. | 500 g), coarsely chopped

3¼ cups | 740 mL coconut milk

6 cups | 1.5 L vegetable stock

2 tsp. | 10 mL fresh lime juice

This is one of my sister's favorites. It's easy, flavorful and very rich.

METHOD

Over medium heat, sauté the shallots in olive oil for 3–4 minutes.

Add all of the spices and sauté another minute.

Add the spinach and cook until it is all wilted.

Add the coconut milk and stock, and simmer 15 minutes.

Add the lime juice and serve.

PER SERVING

326	Calories
24 g	Fat (63.6% calories from fat)
7 g	Protein
24 g	Carbohydrate
5 g	Dietary Fiber
1 mg	Cholesterol
1238 mg	Sodium

SERVES 10 | PARVE • DON'T FREEZE

Kale and Pasta Soup

1 small yellow onion, peeled and coarsely chopped

2–4 cloves garlic (2 tsp. | 10 mL), crushed

2 stalks celery, coarsely diced

2 Tbsp. | 25 mL olive oil

8 cups | 2 L stock

1 tsp. | 5 mL salt

¼ tsp. | 1 mL black pepper

¼ tsp. | 1 mL dried basil

1 can (16 oz. or 19 oz. | 540 mL) chickpeas, rinsed and drained

½ lb. | 250 g kale, cut into strips

1 cup | 250 mL farfallini pasta

1 medium red pepper, roasted and cut into strips

You don't need to purée this, so leave out that step if you like. Puréeing the soup gives it a nice, thick consistency.

METHOD

Over medium heat, sauté the onion, garlic and celery in olive oil for 3 minutes.

Add stock, salt, pepper, basil and chickpeas. Cover and bring to a boil. Reduce heat and simmer for 25 minutes on medium-low.

Purée the soup. See *Puréeing Soup* on page 9 in the Techniques section.

Return to the pot and bring the soup back to a boil. Add the kale and pasta and simmer for 4–10 minutes, until pasta is tender. The time will vary depending on pasta size—check the package instructions.

Add the pepper and simmer another 2–3 minutes.

PER SERVING

215	Calories
6 g	Fat (23.6% calories from fat)
8 g	Protein
34 g	Carbohydrate
5 g	Dietary Fiber
0 mg	Cholesterol
1977 mg	Sodium

SERVES 8 | PARVE · DON'T FREEZE

Cauliflower Corn Chowder

1 small yellow onion, peeled and finely chopped

2 Tbsp. | 25 mL olive oil

1½ lbs. | 750 g cauliflower, coarsely chopped
(reserve 2 cups | 500 mL florets)

5 cups | 1.25 L stock

1¼ tsp. | 6 mL salt

¼ tsp. | 1 mL black pepper

1 can (28 oz. | 796 mL) creamed corn

1 cup | 250 mL frozen corn kernels

Cauliflower and corn go incredibly well together. Keeping some of the cauliflower out until the last ten minutes allows for a good contrast in texture.

METHOD

Over medium heat, sauté the onion in olive oil for 3–4 minutes, until it starts to wilt.

Add the cauliflower (reserving the 2 cups | 500 mL of florets), stock, salt and pepper and bring to a boil, covered. Reduce heat to medium-low and simmer for 20 minutes, until all the vegetables are tender.

Add all of the corn and the reserved cauliflower florets. Cook another 10 minutes (until cauliflower is just tender, but not mushy).

PER SERVING

159	Calories
5 g	Fat (24.3% calories from fat)
5 g	Protein
29 g	Carbohydrate
4 g	Dietary Fiber
0 mg	Cholesterol
1570 mg	Sodium

SERVES 8 | PARVE • FREEZES

Tomato Broth with Julienne Vegetables

5 cups | 1.25 L stock

1 cup | 250 mL tomato juice, low-sodium

1 clove garlic (½ tsp. | 2 mL), crushed

½ small carrot, peeled and cut into matchsticks

½ small red onion, peeled and cut into thin strips

½ stalk celery, cut into matchsticks

¼ small bulb fennel, cut into thin strips

2 small Roma (Italian plum) tomatoes, cored, seeded and cut into thin strips

½ small red pepper, cored, seeded and cut into matchsticks

½ small zucchini, cut into thin strips

1½ tsp. | 7 mL salt

¼ tsp. | 1 mL black pepper

1 Tbsp. | 15 mL fresh oregano, chopped

This low-calorie soup is an elegant starter. I use tomato juice and stock because I like the light tomato broth this combination produces.

METHOD

Over high heat, bring stock, tomato juice and garlic to a boil in a covered soup pot. Turn the heat down so the soup simmers gently and add the carrot, onion, celery and fennel and simmer 8–10 minutes.

Add tomatoes, red pepper, zucchini, salt and pepper and simmer another 5 minutes.

Add fresh oregano just before serving.

PER SERVING

45	Calories
1g Fat	(20.3% calories from fat)
2 g	Protein
7 g	Carbohydrate
2 g	Dietary Fiber
0 mg	Cholesterol
1787 mg	Sodium

SERVES 6 | PARVE • FREEZES • PASSOVER

Tomato Rice Soup

1 stalk celery, finely diced

½ small yellow onion, peeled and finely diced

1 small carrot, peeled and finely diced

2 Tbsp. | 25 mL olive oil

5 cups | 1.25 L stock

1 tsp. | 5 mL granulated sugar

1 tsp. | 5 mL salt

¼ tsp. | 1 mL black pepper

1 cup | 250 mL canned diced tomatoes

1 cup | 250 mL canned crushed tomatoes

⅓ cup | 75 mL white rice

Tomato rice soups generally don't have other vegetables in them, but I like the addition of carrots, onions and celery. I dice them into ⅛-inch (3-mm) dice, but if you prefer you can shred them and they will dissolve into the soup a little more.

METHOD

Over medium-low heat, sauté vegetables in olive oil for 8–10 minutes, until they are soft, but not browned.

Add the stock, granulated sugar, salt, pepper and tomatoes. Cover and bring to a boil over high heat. Reduce heat and simmer for 20 minutes over medium-low.

Add rice and continue cooking, covered, for 30 minutes or until the rice is tender.

PER SERVING

144	Calories
6 g	Fat (35.2% calories from fat)
3 g	Protein
20 g	Carbohydrate
2 g	Dietary Fiber
0 mg	Cholesterol
1664 mg	Sodium

SERVES 6 | PARVE · FREEZES

Mushroom and Potato Soup

1 small yellow onion, peeled and finely chopped

1 small carrot, peeled and finely chopped

½ stalk celery, finely chopped

2 Tbsp. | 25 mL olive oil

1 lb. | 500 g button mushrooms, sliced ¼ inch | 5 mm thick

4–6 cloves garlic (1 Tbsp. | 15 mL), crushed

½ tsp. | 2 mL black pepper

1 tsp. | 5 mL salt

2 tsp. | 10 mL fresh thyme leaves

2–3 medium red potatoes (1 lb. | 500 g), peeled and cubed

6 cups | 1.5 L stock

Mushrooms, garlic and thyme are natural partners. Potatoes make a wonderful addition to this classic combo.

METHOD

Over medium-low heat, sauté onion, carrot and celery in olive oil for 3–5 minutes.

Add mushrooms, garlic, pepper, salt and thyme and sauté 10 minutes over medium-high heat, until the mushrooms start to release their juices.

Add potatoes and stock, cover, turn heat up and bring to a boil. Reduce heat and simmer for 20 minutes on medium-low.

PER SERVING

153	Calories
6 g	Fat (33.4% calories from fat)
5 g	Protein
22 g	Carbohydrate
3 g	Dietary Fiber
0 mg	Cholesterol
1854 mg	Sodium

SERVES 6 | PARVE · FREEZES · PASSOVER

Mushroom Barley Soup

1 large yellow onion, peeled and finely chopped

2 stalks celery, finely chopped

2 Tbsp. | 25 mL olive oil

1½ lbs. | 750 g mushrooms, washed and sliced

8 cups | 2 L vegetable stock

1½ tsp. | 7 mL salt

¼ tsp. | 1 mL black pepper

½ cup | 125 mL pearl barley, rinsed

Another simple, filling soup. You can add any vegetables you like. Depending on the type of barley you use, the cooking time will vary. If the soup needs to cook longer, you may need to add some extra water to replace the liquid that evaporates.

METHOD

Sauté onion and celery in olive oil 4–5 minutes over medium-high heat.

When onion and celery are wilted, add the sliced mushrooms. Continue to stir and cook for 5–6 minutes, until the mushrooms start to release their juices.

Add the stock, salt and pepper, cover and bring to a boil.

Add the rinsed barley, reduce heat and simmer for 25–35 minutes on medium-low heat, until barley is soft and tender.

Adjust salt and pepper seasoning.

PER SERVING

185	Calories
5 g	Fat (24.9% calories from fat)
7 g	Protein
29 g	Carbohydrate
5 g	Dietary Fiber
2 mg	Cholesterol
1362 mg	Sodium

SERVES 12 | PARVE · FREEZES

Mushroom Eggdrop Soup

½ small yellow onion, peeled and cut into ¼-inch | 5-mm strips

2 Tbsp. | 25 mL olive oil

10 oz. | 300 g button mushrooms, sliced ¼ inch | 5 mm thick

1–2 cloves garlic (1 tsp. | 5 mL), crushed

½ tsp. | 2 mL fresh ginger, finely minced

5 cups | 1.25 L stock

¼ tsp. | 1 mL black pepper

2 Tbsp. | 25 mL soy sauce

¼ cup | 50 mL canned water chestnuts, sliced into ⅛- x ½-inch (3-mm x 1-cm) sticks

2 Tbsp. | 25 mL canned bamboo shoots

1–2 medium green onions (scallions), thinly sliced

½ cup | 125 mL bean sprouts (1 oz. | 25 g)

½ cup | 125 mL cold water

2 Tbsp. | 25 mL cornstarch

2 eggs

1 Tbsp. | 15 mL dark sesame oil

This is a very rich soup. Instead of the 4 servings I suggest, it will easily stretch to 6–8 servings as an appetizer. Make sure the sesame oil is a dark, toasted Asian style —the flavor can't be beat!

METHOD

Over medium-low heat, sauté the onion in olive oil for 5 minutes, until wilted, not browned.

Add the mushrooms and continue to sauté until they release their juices, 8–10 minutes.

Add garlic and ginger and sauté for 30 seconds, stirring constantly.

Add stock, black pepper and soy sauce, cover and turn the heat up to high to bring the soup to a boil. Reduce heat and simmer for another 5 minutes on medium-low.

Add all of the vegetables and bring the soup back to a simmer.

In a separate bowl, whisk together the cold water and cornstarch. In another bowl, whisk together the eggs and sesame oil.

Pour the cornstarch/water mixture into the soup and whisk in. Allow the soup to cook 1–2 minutes, thickening up.

Slowly pour the egg/sesame oil mixture into the soup in a thin stream. Wait 10 seconds and stir, breaking up the long streams of cooked egg.

PER SERVING	
192	Calories
14 g	Fat (63.7% calories from fat)
7 g	Protein
11 g	Carbohydrate
2 g	Dietary Fiber
94 mg	Cholesterol
2404 mg	Sodium

SERVES 4 | PARVE • DON'T FREEZE

Eight-Mushroom Soup

1 oz. | 25 g dried mushrooms, (oyster, porcini, chanterelle and shiitake)

2 cups | 500 mL cold water

1 medium yellow onion, peeled and finely chopped

3 Tbsp. | 45 mL olive oil

3 oz. | 75 g oyster mushrooms, torn into large chunks

3 oz. | 75 g button mushrooms, quartered

5 oz. | 150 g crimini mushrooms, quartered

4 oz. | 125 g portobello mushrooms, cut into large chunks

4–6 cloves garlic (1 Tbsp. | 15 mL), crushed

¼ cup | 50 mL dry red wine

1 cup | 250 mL stock

1 tsp. | 5 mL salt

¼ tsp. | 1 mL black pepper

chopped chives for garnish

This soup celebrates mushrooms. The liquid used for soaking the dried mushrooms adds an amazing richness and there are few other flavors to overshadow the mushrooms themselves. You can substitute the mushrooms in this recipe with any that you prefer.

METHOD

Rinse the dried mushrooms well, getting rid of any dust or dirt, and place them in a bowl. Bring the water to a boil and pour over the mushrooms. Allow to cool. Use a slotted spoon to remove the mushrooms and reserve the liquid. If the mushrooms are whole, cut them into chunks.

Over medium-low heat, sauté onion in olive oil for 10 minutes, until it starts to caramelize.

Add fresh mushrooms and sauté over medium heat for 8 minutes. The mushrooms will start to release their juices.

Add rehydrated dried mushrooms and garlic and sauté another 2–3 minutes.

Increase heat to high and add the red wine. Cook 2–3 minutes, allowing the wine to reduce.

Slowly pour in the liquid left over from rehydrating the dried mushrooms. Make sure to leave any residue in the bottom of the bowl, or pour it all through cheesecloth. Add the stock, salt and pepper, cover and bring soup to a boil. Reduce heat and simmer for 15 minutes.

Garnish with chopped chives.

PER SERVING

120	Calories
7 g	Fat (53.8% calories from fat)
3 g	Protein
11 g	Carbohydrate
2 g	Dietary Fiber
0 mg	Cholesterol
620 mg	Sodium

SERVES 6 | PARVE · FREEZES

Pumpkin and Black Bean Soup

1 small yellow onion, peeled and finely chopped

2 Tbsp. | 25 mL olive oil

1–2 cloves garlic (1 tsp. | 5 mL), crushed

1 Tbsp. | 15 mL ground cumin

2 tsp. | 10 mL ground coriander

1½ tsp. | 7 mL salt

¼ tsp. | 1 mL black pepper

1 can (28 oz. | 798 mL) pumpkin

1 can (16 oz. or 19 oz. | 540 mL) black beans, rinsed and drained

6 cups | 1.5 L stock

Using canned pumpkin is a great time-saver. If you are using pumpkins from your garden, just cut them in half and roast them in the oven until tender.

METHOD

Over medium-low heat, sauté onion in olive oil for 7–9 minutes, until very tender, but not browned.

Add garlic and spices and sauté another 30 seconds, stirring constantly.

Add canned pumpkin, black beans and stock. Make sure everything is well stirred and incorporated. Cover and bring to a boil. Reduce heat and simmer gently for 20 minutes.

PER SERVING

147	Calories
5 g	Fat (31.4% calories from fat)
6 g	Protein
20 g	Carbohydrate
7 g	Dietary Fiber
0 mg	Cholesterol
1726 mg	Sodium

SERVES 8 | PARVE • FREEZES

❧ Middle Eastern Squash and Couscous Soup

1 small yellow onion, peeled and finely chopped

3 Tbsp. | 45 mL olive oil

2–4 cloves garlic (2 tsp. | 10 mL), crushed

1 tsp. | 5 mL salt

¼ tsp. | 1 mL black pepper

¼ tsp. | 1 mL chili powder

½ tsp. | 2 mL ground ginger

½ tsp. | 2 mL cumin

¼ tsp. | 1 mL ground nutmeg

½ tsp. | 2 mL paprika

½ tsp. | 2 mL coriander

1 medium acorn squash (about ¾ lb. | 375 g), peeled, seeded and cubed (½ inch | 1 cm)

1 small carrot, peeled and thinly sliced

8 cups | 2 L stock

1 can (16 oz. or 19 oz. | 540 mL) chickpeas, rinsed and drained

⅓ cup | 75 mL couscous

Your house will smell amazing when you cook this soup. As soon as the spices hit the pan, they release fantastic aromas. The soup tastes just as great as it smells!

METHOD

Over medium heat, sauté the onion in olive oil, 3–4 minutes.

Add spices and cook 1–2 minutes, stirring continuously.

Add squash and carrot and sauté another 3–4 minutes.

Add stock, cover and bring to a boil. Reduce heat and simmer for 30 minutes on medium-low.

Add chickpeas and couscous, and simmer 3–5 minutes. (If you are using a very fine couscous, this may not take as long, and a larger, Israeli-style couscous may need a couple of extra minutes of cooking.)

PER SERVING

200	Calories
7 g	Fat (31.7% calories from fat)
6 g	Protein
28 g	Carbohydrate
5 g	Dietary Fiber
0 mg	Cholesterol
1958 mg	Sodium

SERVES 8 | PARVE · DON'T FREEZE

Kabocha Squash, Tomato and Black Bean Soup

1 small yellow onion, peeled and coarsely chopped

2 Tbsp. | 25 mL olive oil

4–6 cloves garlic (1 Tbsp. | 15 mL), crushed

2 tsp. | 10 mL salt

¼ tsp. | 1 mL black pepper

½ tsp. | 2 mL Chinese five spice powder

¼ tsp. | 1 mL ground ginger

¼ tsp. | 1 mL chili powder

1 tsp. | 5 mL granulated sugar

1 can (28 oz. | 796 mL) diced tomatoes

1 medium kabocha squash flesh (about 1 lb. | 500 g), peeled, seeded and cubed

6 cups | 1.5 L stock

1 can (16 oz. or 19 oz. | 540 mL) black beans, rinsed and drained

Although this soup contains Chinese five spice powder, it doesn't taste like any Chinese food I've ever had. If you can't find kabocha squash, substitute butternut or acorn squash. Or, since the kabocha tastes a lot like a sweet potato, you could try using that as well.

METHOD

Sauté onion in olive oil over medium-low heat for 5–8 minutes, until wilted.

Add garlic, spices and granulated sugar and sauté 30 seconds, stirring constantly.

Add tomatoes, squash, stock and black beans. Cover and bring to a boil over high heat. Reduce temperature and simmer for half an hour, until the squash is tender.

PER SERVING

146	Calories
5 g	Fat (31.2% calories from fat)
6 g	Protein
19 g	Carbohydrate
6 g	Dietary Fiber
0 mg	Cholesterol
1864 mg	Sodium

SERVES 8 | PARVE · FREEZES

❧ Curried Apple and Butternut Squash Soup

½ small yellow onion, peeled and coarsely chopped

2 Tbsp. | 25 mL olive oil

1–2 cloves garlic (1 tsp. | 5 mL), crushed

1 tsp. | 5 mL medium curry powder

½ tsp. | 2 mL ground cumin

¼ tsp. | 1 mL ground coriander

¼ tsp. | 1 mL ground ginger

¼ tsp. | 1 mL ground cinnamon

¼ tsp. | 1 mL ground turmeric

⅛ tsp. | .5 mL ground nutmeg

⅛ tsp. | .5 mL ground cardamom

¼ tsp. | 1 mL black pepper

1 tsp. | 5 mL salt

1 medium butternut squash (1 lb. | 500 g),
peeled, seeded and cut into small chunks

4 cups | 1 L stock

3–4 medium Granny Smith apples (1 lb. | 500 g),
peeled, cored and chopped

I use Granny Smith apples because I like to cut through the curry with acid. If you use an apple that is more sweet than tart, add a spoonful of fresh lemon juice to the soup.

METHOD

Over medium heat, sauté the onion in olive oil for 8–10 minutes. The onion will start to brown and caramelize.

Add all of the spices and seasonings and cook another 30 seconds, stirring constantly.

Add the squash and stock, cover and bring to a boil. Lower the heat and simmer the soup gently for 2 minutes.

Add the apples and simmer the soup for 10 minutes.

Purée the soup. See *Puréeing Soups* on page 9 in the Techniques section.

PER SERVING

179	Calories
8 g	Fat (39.2% calories from fat)
3 g	Protein
26 g	Carbohydrate
4 g	Dietary Fiber
0 mg	Cholesterol
2023 mg	Sodium

SERVES 4 | PARVE • FREEZES

Butternut Squash and Granny Smith Apple Soup

1 large yellow onion, peeled and chopped

2 Tbsp. | 25 mL olive oil

1 tsp. | 5 mL fresh ginger, grated

¼ tsp. | 1 mL ground cinnamon

1 bay leaf

1 tsp. | 5 mL granulated sugar

2 tsp. | 10 mL salt

¼ tsp. | 1 mL black pepper

1 medium butternut squash (about 1 lb. | 500 g), peeled, seeded and cubed

5 cups | 1.25 L stock

2–3 medium Granny Smith apples (1 lb. | 500 g), peeled, cored and cubed

heavy or whipping cream (35%) to finish (optional)

An elegant soup. Serve with chopped fresh raw apple for a crunchy garnish.

METHOD

Over medium heat, sweat the onion in olive oil for approximately 5 minutes.

Add the ginger, cinnamon, bay leaf, granulated sugar, salt and pepper and cook an additional minute, stirring constantly.

Add the squash and stock and bring to a simmer. Add the apples and simmer for approximately 15 minutes.

When the squash is tender, pull out the bay leaf. Purée the soup. See *Puréeing Soups* on page 9 in the Techniques section.

If you like, you can add some cream to smooth the soup out, but I like the sharp tartness of this one without the cream. If you add the cream, use full 35% cream—lower-fat cream will curdle.

PER SERVING

78	Calories
3 g	Fat (36.8% calories from fat)
1 g	Protein
12 g	Carbohydrate
2 g	Dietary Fiber
0 mg	Cholesterol
1171 mg	Sodium

SERVES 10 | PARVE WITHOUT CREAM • FREEZES • PASSOVER

Split Pea Soup

1 medium yellow onion, peeled and finely chopped

1 medium carrot, peeled and finely chopped

1 stalk celery, finely chopped

3 Tbsp. | 45 mL olive oil

4–6 cloves garlic (1 Tbsp. | 15 mL), crushed

2 cups | 500 mL dried green split peas (1 lb. | 500 g), picked through and rinsed well

8 cups | 2 L stock

1 tsp. | 5 mL salt

¼ tsp. | 1 mL black pepper

A traditional split pea soup usually has some smoked meat in it. If you have some leftover smoked turkey, add it for a nice smoky flavor.

METHOD

Over medium-low heat, sweat the vegetables in the olive oil for 10 minutes. They should be wilted but not brown, so make sure your heat isn't too high.

Add the garlic and cook another minute.

Add the split peas and stock, cover and bring to a boil. Reduce heat and simmer gently over medium-low heat for 1¼ hours, or until the peas are cooked and broken down, thickening the soup.

Season with salt and pepper and serve.

PER SERVING

278	Calories
7 g	Fat (21.8% calories from fat)
16 g	Protein
40 g	Carbohydrate
16 g	Dietary Fiber
0 mg	Cholesterol
1772 mg	Sodium

SERVES 8 | PARVE • FREEZES

❧ Lentil Soup #1

1 cup | 250 mL lentils, rinsed well

1 medium potato, peeled and diced small

1 medium carrot, peeled and diced small

2 stalks celery, diced small

1 small yellow onion, peeled and diced small

12–18 cloves garlic (3 Tbsp. | 45 mL), crushed

10 cups | 2.5 L water

1 tsp. | 5 mL salt

¼ tsp. | 1 mL black pepper

Undoubtedly the easiest and probably the healthiest soup I make. Not to mention that it tastes amazingly good. I like to dice the vegetables into very small cubes (¼ inch / 5 mm square) so that everything is approximately the same size as the cooked lentils, but it would work just as well to cut everything into larger chunks to save on prep time.

METHOD

Put everything into a soup pot. Cover and bring to a boil over high heat. Reduce heat to medium and simmer over medium-low until lentils are tender, approximately half an hour.

Check soup for seasoning.

PER SERVING

106	Calories
trace	Fat (2.4% calories from fat)
7 g	Protein
20 g	Carbohydrate
8 g	Dietary Fiber
0 mg	Cholesterol
237 mg	Sodium

SERVES 10 | PARVE · FREEZES

Lentil Soup #2

1 small yellow onion, peeled and finely chopped

4–6 cloves garlic (1 Tbsp. | 15 mL), crushed

1 Tbsp. | 15 mL ground cumin

2 tsp. | 10 mL ground coriander

½ tsp. | 2 mL ground cinnamon

1 cup | 250 mL dry red wine

5 cups | 1.25 L water

1 can (28 oz. | 796 mL) diced tomatoes

¾ cup | 175 mL lentils, picked through and rinsed well

1 stalk celery, finely chopped

1 small carrot, peeled and finely chopped

1½ tsp. | 7 mL salt

¼ tsp. | 1 mL black pepper

1 Tbsp. | 15 mL granulated sugar

This is a hearty, winey, flavorful vegetarian soup that is simple to prepare. With some fresh, crusty bread you have a great meal.

METHOD

Put all the ingredients into a soup pot. With the lid on, bring the soup to a boil over high heat. Reduce heat to medium-low, and simmer for 50 minutes, or until all vegetables and lentils are tender.

PER SERVING

136	Calories
1 g	Fat (4.6% calories from fat)
8 g	Protein
22 g	Carbohydrate
8 g	Dietary Fiber
0 mg	Cholesterol
587 mg	Sodium

SERVES 8 | PARVE • FREEZES

Red Lentil Soup

1 medium yellow onion, peeled and finely chopped

2 Tbsp. | 25 mL olive oil

4–6 cloves garlic (1 Tbsp. | 15 mL), ground

⅛ tsp. | .5 mL chili powder

1 tsp. | 5 mL ground cumin

1½ tsp. | 7 mL salt

¼ tsp. | 1 mL black pepper

¾ cup | 175 mL red lentils, rinsed well

6 cups | 1.5 L stock

1 small butternut squash (½ lb. | 250 g), peeled and diced (⅓ inch | 8 mm)

3 cups | 750 mL firmly packed baby spinach (½ lb. | 250 g), washed and dried

The red lentils will melt as they cook, making a thicker soup. I like butternut squash, but you can use any hard-skinned squash you like.

METHOD

Over medium heat, sweat the onion in olive oil for approximately 5 minutes.

Add all of the seasonings and cook another 1–2 minutes.

Add the lentils and the stock and bring to a simmer. Simmer the soup on medium-low heat for 20 minutes.

Add the squash and simmer another 15 minutes.

Add the spinach and cook another 3–5 minutes.

PER SERVING

69	Calories
4 g	Fat (54.2% calories from fat)
2 g	Protein
7 g	Carbohydrate
1 g	Dietary Fiber
0 mg	Cholesterol
1515 mg	Sodium

SERVES 8 | PARVE • FREEZES

Red Lentil and Tomato Soup

4–6 cloves garlic (1 Tbsp. | 15 mL), crushed

1 small yellow onion, peeled and finely chopped

½ cup | 125 mL dry red wine

4 cups | 1 L water

2 stalks celery, thinly sliced

1 medium carrot, peeled, cut in half and thinly sliced

½ cup | 125 mL red lentils, picked through and rinsed well

1½ tsp. | 7 mL salt

¼ tsp. | 1 mL black pepper

1 can (28 oz. | 796 mL) diced tomatoes

1 bay leaf

This soup is good as is but if you want to add some different flavors, try adding ½ tsp. (2 mL) of dried oregano, basil or thyme. Serve with garlic bread for a great lunch on a cold weekend.

METHOD

Put everything into a pot. Cover and bring to a boil over high heat. Reduce the heat and simmer gently for 45 minutes on medium-low.

Remove bay leaf and serve.

PER SERVING

126	Calories
1 g	Fat (5.2% calories from fat)
7 g	Protein
22 g	Carbohydrate
8 g	Dietary Fiber
0 mg	Cholesterol
587 mg	Sodium

SERVES 6 | PARVE • FREEZES

Rice and Bean Soup

1 medium yellow onion, peeled and finely chopped

1 medium green bell pepper, cored, seeded and cut into ¼-inch (5-mm) dice

2–3 stalks celery, cut into ¼-inch | 5-mm dice

2 Tbsp. | 25 mL olive oil

1½ tsp. | 7 mL salt

¼ tsp. | 1 mL black pepper

1 tsp. | 5 mL paprika

2 tsp. | 10 mL chili powder

2 bay leaves

1–2 cloves garlic (1 tsp. | 5 mL), crushed

3 oz. | 75 g white rice

1 can (16 oz. or 19 oz. | 540 mL) black beans, rinsed and drained

7 cups | 1.75 L stock

I've spent only one short weekend in New Orleans, but this recipe reminds me of something I may have had there. Whether or not it really is true New Orleans cooking, it tastes great!

METHOD

Over medium heat, sauté the onion, green pepper and celery in olive oil for 10 minutes, stirring occasionally.

Add all of the spices and sauté 30 seconds, stirring constantly.

Add the rice and sauté another 30 seconds, stirring to coat the rice with the oil and spices.

Add the black beans and stock, cover and bring to a boil over high heat. Reduce heat and simmer on medium-low for 20–25 minutes, or until the rice is tender.

PER SERVING

164	Calories
5 g	Fat (28.5% calories from fat)
6 g	Protein
23 g	Carbohydrate
5 g	Dietary Fiber
0 mg	Cholesterol
1927 mg	Sodium

SERVES 8 | PARVE • FREEZES

Minestrone Soup

½ small yellow onion, coarsely chopped

1 stalk celery, sliced ¼ inch | 5 mm thick

1 small carrot, peeled, cut in half and sliced
¼ inch | 5 mm thick

1 cup | 250 mL cabbage (firmly packed), sliced into
¼-inch | 5 mm strips

2 Tbsp. | 25 mL olive oil

1–2 cloves garlic (1 tsp. | 5 mL), crushed

2 tsp. | 10 mL salt

¼ tsp. | 1 mL black pepper

¾ tsp. | 4 mL dried oregano

½ tsp. | 2 mL dried basil

1 cup | 250 mL tomato juice, low-sodium

6 cups | 1.5 L stock

1 can (16 oz. or 19 oz. | 540 mL) kidney beans,
rinsed and drained

¾ cup | 175 mL macaroni

*This is my version of minestrone soup. I like the com-
bination of tomato juice and stock—it achieves a nice,
light tomato broth.*

METHOD

Over medium-low heat, sauté the vegetables in olive oil for
5–7 minutes, until they are wilted, but not browned.

Add the garlic and spices and sauté another 30 seconds,
stirring constantly.

Add tomato juice and stock, cover and turn the heat up to
bring the soup to a boil.

Add the kidney beans and pasta, reduce heat so that the
soup simmers gently and cook another 15 minutes, until
the pasta is just tender. Be careful not to cook the pasta too
long or it will be mushy. If you use a different pasta shape,
the cooking time will vary—check package directions for
cooking times.

PER SERVING

161	Calories
5 g	Fat (25.9% calories from fat)
7 g	Protein
24 g	Carbohydrate
6 g	Dietary Fiber
0 mg	Cholesterol
1890 mg	Sodium

SERVES 8 | PARVE · FREEZES

Mexican Rice and Black Bean Soup

1 small yellow onion, peeled and finely chopped

2 whole jalapeno peppers, cored, seeded and finely chopped

2 Tbsp. | 25 mL olive oil

2–4 cloves garlic (2 tsp. | 10 mL), crushed

1 tsp. | 5 mL cumin

1 tsp. | 5 mL coriander

½ tsp. | 2 mL chili powder

1 tsp. | 5 mL paprika

1 tsp. | 5 mL salt

¼ tsp. | 1 mL black pepper

1 can (5½ oz. | 156 mL) tomato paste

1 can (28 oz. | 796 mL) diced tomatoes

7 cups | 1.75 L water

¾ cup | 175 mL white rice

1 can (12 oz. | 350 mL) corn kernels, drained

1 can (16 oz. or 19 oz. | 540 mL) black beans, rinsed and drained

1 Tbsp. | 15 mL cilantro, chopped

grated cheddar cheese and sour cream for garnish

Garnish this soup with cheddar cheese and sour cream.

METHOD

Over medium-high heat, sauté the onion and jalapeno in olive oil for 3–4 minutes.

Add all of the spices, except the cilantro, and sauté another 1–2 minutes.

Add the tomato paste and canned tomatoes and cook another 2–3 minutes.

Add water, cover and bring to a boil. Reduce heat and simmer 20 minutes on medium-low.

Add rice and simmer another 10 minutes, until rice is tender.

Add corn and beans and allow to heat through, 3–5 minutes.

Right before serving, add the cilantro.

PER SERVING

162	Calories
4 g	Fat (19.5% calories from fat)
5 g	Protein
28 g	Carbohydrate
5 g	Dietary Fiber
0 mg	Cholesterol
582 mg	Sodium

SERVES 10 | PARVE WITHOUT CHEESE OR SOUR CREAM • FREEZES

Italian Bean Soup

1 small white onion, finely chopped

1 Tbsp. | 15 mL olive oil

8–12 cloves garlic (2 Tbsp. | 25 mL), minced

1 small rutabaga (about ¼ lb. | 125 g), peeled and cut into ⅓-inch | 8-mm cubes

10 cups | 2.5 L stock

1 cup | 250 mL macaroni

1 can (16 oz. or 19 oz. | 540 mL) white beans, rinsed and drained

1 small zucchini, sliced ¼ inch | 5 mm thick

1 tsp. | 5 mL salt

¼ tsp. | 1 mL black pepper

1 tsp. | 5 mL dried basil

2 cups | 500 mL firmly packed spinach leaves (¼ lb. | 125 g), coarsely chopped

1 medium red pepper, roasted, peeled and cut into strips

This is another great take on minestrone—in fact, in our restaurant we call it White Minestrone.

METHOD

Sauté onion in olive oil over medium heat for 3–4 minutes.

Add garlic and continue to sauté, while stirring, for another minute.

Add rutabaga and stock, cover and bring to a boil. Allow to simmer on low heat for 15 minutes.

Add the macaroni and simmer for another 5 minutes.

Add beans, zucchini, salt, pepper and basil and simmer for an additional 3 minutes.

Add spinach and pepper and cook another minute, to warm everything.

Check for seasoning and serve!

PER SERVING

159	Calories
3 g	Fat (9.3% calories from fat)
8 g	Protein
26 g	Carbohydrate
4 g	Dietary Fiber
0 mg	Cholesterol
1711 mg	Sodium

SERVES 10 | DAIRY • FREEZES

Bean and Barley Soup

1 large carrot, peeled and shredded

1 small yellow onion, peeled and finely chopped

2 stalks celery, finely chopped

½ cup | 125 mL barley

6 oz. | 175 g mushrooms, sliced ¼ inch | 5 mm thick

1 can (16 oz. or 19 oz. | 540 mL) black beans,
rinsed and drained

1 can (16 oz. or 19 oz. | 540 mL) white beans,
rinsed and drained

1 can (16 oz. or 19 oz. | 540 mL) Romano (or kidney)
beans, rinsed and drained

1 tsp. | 5 mL salt

¼ tsp. | 1 mL black pepper

12 cups | 3 L stock

*This is a filling, easy and healthy soup. Just put every-
thing into a pot, stir occasionally and enjoy!*

METHOD
Place everything in a soup pot and cover. Over medium
heat, bring to a boil and simmer 45 minutes, or until the
barley is tender.

PER SERVING

183	Calories
2 g	Fat (8.4% calories from fat)
10 g	Protein
32 g	Carbohydrate
8 g	Dietary Fiber
0 mg	Cholesterol
1558 mg	Sodium

SERVES 14 | PARVE • FREEZES

❧ Black Bean Soup

1 small carrot, peeled and finely chopped

2 stalks celery, finely chopped

1–2 small shallots (1½ oz. | 40 g), peeled and finely chopped

1 whole jalapeno, cored, seeded and finely diced

2 Tbsp. | 25 mL olive oil

2–4 cloves garlic (2 tsp. | 10 mL), crushed

1 tsp. | 5 mL ground cumin

1 tsp. | 5 mL salt

¼ tsp. | 1 mL black pepper

2 cans black beans (38 oz. | 1080 mL), rinsed and drained

4 cups | 1 L stock

sour cream, grated cheddar cheese and chopped chives for garnish

If you like, you can reserve some of the black beans and add them after the soup has been puréed. The contrast in textures is nice.

METHOD

Over medium heat, sauté carrot, celery, shallots and jalapeno in olive oil for 3–5 minutes, stirring constantly.

Add garlic, cumin, salt and pepper and continue cooking 1–2 minutes, while stirring.

Add beans and stock, cover and bring to a boil and simmer 15 minutes on medium-low.

Purée the soup (see *Puréeing Soups* on page 9 in the Techniques section) and return to the stove. Simmer another 20–25 minutes, stirring occasionally.

Serve garnished with sour cream, grated cheddar cheese and chopped chives.

PER SERVING

165	Calories
5 g	Fat (28.2% calories from fat)
8 g	Protein
21 g	Carbohydrate
8 g	Dietary Fiber
0 mg	Cholesterol
1427 mg	Sodium

SERVES 8 | PARVE WITHOUT SOUR CREAM AND CHEESE • FREEZES

Hot and Sour Soup

¼ oz. | 5 g dried shiitake mushrooms

1 cup | 250 mL boiling water

1 small carrot, peeled and cut into matchsticks

4 cups | 1 L stock

1 cup | 250 mL bean sprouts

¼ lb. | 125 g firm tofu, cut into ½-inch | 1-cm cubes

⅛ cup | 25 mL bamboo shoots

⅛ cup | 25 mL water chestnuts, cut into matchsticks

2 Tbsp. | 25 mL soy sauce

1½ tsp. | 7 mL sambal oelek (chili sauce)

¼ tsp. | 1 mL black pepper

3 Tbsp. | 45 mL cornstarch

1 cup | 250 mL cold water

2 eggs

1 Tbsp. | 15 mL toasted sesame oil

3 Tbsp. | 45 mL rice wine vinegar

1–2 green onions (scallions), sliced very thin

Using the soaking liquid from the shiitake mushrooms adds amazing flavor to the soup. It's a little spicy and a little sour. Add or remove the chili sauce and vinegar to suit your taste.

METHOD

Rinse the dried shiitake mushrooms well and put them in a bowl. Pour the boiling water over them and set aside, covered, until the mushrooms have cooled. When cool enough to handle, take them out of the water. If the mushrooms are whole, take off the stems and discard, then slice the mushroom caps into thin strips.

Slowly pour the remaining mushroom water into the soup pot, being careful to leave any residue in the bottom of the bowl. Add the carrot and stock to the pot, cover and bring to a boil.

When the soup has boiled, turn the heat down so it is simmering gently and add the bean sprouts, mushrooms, tofu, bamboo shoots, water chestnuts, soy sauce, sambal oelek and black pepper and simmer for 1–2 minutes.

In a separate bowl, whisk together the cornstarch and cold water. Pour into the soup and mix well. Allow soup to cook another 1–2 minutes, until it has thickened.

In another bowl, whisk together the eggs and sesame oil. In a slow, thin stream pour the mixture into the soup and wait 10 seconds before stirring. Add the vinegar. Garnish with green onions and serve.

PER SERVING

161	Calories
5 g	Fat (31.0% calories from fat)
8 g	Protein
15 g	Carbohydrate
2 g	Dietary Fiber
94 mg	Cholesterol
2040 mg	Sodium

SERVES 4 | PARVE · DON'T FREEZE

Peanut Soup

1 small yellow onion, peeled and finely chopped

2 Tbsp. | 25 mL olive oil

2–4 cloves garlic (2 tsp. | 10 mL), crushed

1 can (28 oz. | 796 mL) diced tomatoes

4 cups | 1 L stock

1 cup | 250 mL smooth peanut butter

1 Tbsp. | 15 mL hot sauce

1–2 green onions (scallions), thinly sliced

½ cup | 125 mL raw, unsalted peanuts, chopped

½ tsp. | 2 mL salt

¼ tsp. | 1 mL black pepper

1 Tbsp. | 15 mL fresh lime juice

The hot sauce, tomatoes and lime juice cut the richness of the peanut butter. Serve extras of all these so your guests can make it as hot and sour as they like.

METHOD

Sauté onion in olive oil over medium heat for 5–7 minutes.

Add garlic and sauté another 30 seconds, stirring constantly.

Add tomatoes, stock and peanut butter, mix well, cover and turn heat up to bring soup to a boil. Once it reaches the boiling point, reduce heat to medium-low and simmer gently for 15 minutes.

Add hot sauce, green onions, peanuts, salt, pepper and lime juice.

PER SERVING

320	Calories
26 g	Fat (68.0% calories from fat)
13 g	Protein
15 g	Carbohydrate
4 g	Dietary Fiber
0 mg	Cholesterol
1084 mg	Sodium

SERVES 8 | PARVE • DON'T FREEZE

Green Pea and Mint Soup

1 small yellow onion, peeled and coarsely chopped

1 Tbsp. | 15 mL olive oil

4 cups | 1 L frozen peas (1 lb. | 500 g), thawed

4 cups | 1 L stock

1 tsp. | 5 mL salt

¼ tsp. | 1 mL black pepper

1 cup | 250 mL fresh mint leaves (firmly packed)

The English often pair peas with mint and this soup borrows from that tradition. Initially, I meant for this soup to be served hot but it's great cold as well. Try it both ways and see which you prefer.

METHOD

Sauté the onion in olive oil over medium-low heat for 6–7 minutes, just until softened, not browned.

Add the peas, stock, salt and pepper, cover and bring to a boil. Lower heat and simmer for 1–2 minutes only, allowing the peas to be heated, but not cooked so long they lose their color.

Take the soup off the heat and add the mint.

Purée the soup. See *Puréeing Soups* on page 9 in the Techniques section.

If serving hot, reheat if necessary and serve right away. For a cold soup, transfer to a bowl and refrigerate a minimum of 4 hours before serving.

PER SERVING

102	Calories
3 g	Fat (28.8% calories from fat)
5 g	Protein
13 g	Carbohydrate
4 g	Dietary Fiber
0 mg	Cholesterol
1431 mg	Sodium

SERVES 6 | PARVE • DON'T FREEZE

Gazpacho

3 medium Roma (Italian plum) tomatoes, cored and seeded

1 medium red pepper, cored and seeded

½ medium red onion, peeled

1 large English (long seedless) cucumber, peeled and seeded

1–2 cloves garlic (1 tsp. | 5 mL), crushed

1 Tbsp. | 15 mL red wine vinegar

2 Tbsp. | 25 mL olive oil

1½ tsp. | 7 mL salt

¼ tsp. | 1 mL black pepper

1 tsp. | 5 mL hot sauce

½ cup | 125 mL tomato juice, low-sodium

2 Tbsp. | 25 mL fresh chives, finely chopped

2 Tbsp. | 25 mL fresh parsley, finely chopped

Keep a pitcher of this in the fridge during the hottest part of summer. There is no heating involved, and this soup, with some good French bread, will make a perfect, refreshing meal when you don't feel like cooking.

METHOD

Dice a third of the tomatoes, red pepper, onion and cucumber into ¼-inch-square (5-mm-square) uniform pieces and set aside.

In a food processor or blender, purée the remaining two-thirds of the vegetables and all of the garlic, red wine vinegar, olive oil, salt, pepper, hot sauce and tomato juice until the mixture is as smooth as possible. If the soup doesn't have enough liquid, add some extra tomato juice.

Transfer gazpacho into a bowl and stir in the reserved diced vegetables and the herbs. Chill, covered, for at least 4 hours. It's better chilled overnight, allowing all of the flavors to blend. You can also dish up the puréed soup and leave the small, diced vegetables out of the mixture to be used as a garnish when serving.

PER SERVING

111	Calories
7 g	Fat (54.1% calories from fat)
2 g	Protein
12 g	Carbohydrate
3 g	Dietary Fiber
0 mg	Cholesterol
843 mg	Sodium

SERVES 4 | PARVE · DON'T FREEZE · PASSOVER

Dairy Soups

Baba's Break-the-Fast Soup

1 small yellow onion, peeled and diced

3 Tbsp. | 45 mL olive oil

1 small carrot, peeled and diced small

1 stalk celery, diced small

½ small parsnip, peeled and diced

6 cups | 1.5 L stock

1 medium red potato, peeled and diced

1½ cups | 375 mL green beans, trimmed and cut into 1-inch | 2.5-cm pieces

¼ lb. | 125 g button mushrooms, sliced ¼ inch | 5 mm thick

3 Tbsp. | 45 mL all-purpose flour

3 cups | 750 mL 2% milk

2 oz. | 50 g thin soup noodles

1 Tbsp. | 15 mL fresh dill, finely chopped

1 tsp. | 5 mL salt

¼ tsp. | 1 mL black pepper

My grandmother made a soup similar to this one every year for breaking the Yom Kipper fast. I've replicated it to the best of my abilities using my memories of her wonderful soup. Her vegetables may have varied, depending on what her garden had to offer. You can vary them too, if you have a great crop!

METHOD

Over medium-low heat, sauté the onion in olive oil for 2–3 minutes, stirring as it cooks. Add the carrot, celery and parsnip and continue cooking another 2–3 minutes.

Add the stock and potato, cover and bring to a boil over high heat. Add the beans and mushrooms, reduce heat to medium-low and allow to simmer gently for 15 minutes.

In a separate bowl, whisk together the flour and milk. Make sure the mixture is well blended and there are no lumps. Whisk the mixture into the soup and add the noodles. Bring the soup back up to a simmer.

Cook until the noodles are tender and add the dill, salt and pepper.

PER SERVING

130	Calories
6 g	Fat (42.4% calories from fat)
5 g	Protein
14 g	Carbohydrate
2 g	Dietary Fiber
5 mg	Cholesterol
1149 mg	Sodium

SERVES 10 | DAIRY · FREEZES

Pepper Pot Soup

1 medium yellow onion, peeled and shredded

2 small carrots, peeled and grated

1 large or 2 small green peppers, seeded and finely chopped

3 Tbsp. | 45 mL olive oil

2 medium red potatoes, peeled and shredded

5 cups | 1.25 mL stock

1 cup | 250 mL half-and-half

2 cups | 500 mL 2% milk

3 Tbsp. | 45 mL all-purpose flour

2 tsp. | 10 mL salt

1 tsp. | 5 mL black pepper

Using a food processor to shred the vegetables makes the preparation for this soup quick. A friend likes to add a lot of extra black pepper, but taste it first. It makes me sneeze as it is!

METHOD

Sweat onion, carrots and pepper in olive oil over medium heat for approximately 8–10 minutes.

Add the potatoes and stock, cover and bring to a boil. Reduce heat and simmer for 10 minutes on medium-low.

In a separate bowl, whisk together the half-and-half, milk and flour. Make sure there are no lumps. Whisk this mixture into the soup. Allow the soup to come back to a simmer and cook another 2–3 minutes, allowing the flour to cook and the soup to thicken. Season with salt and pepper.

PER SERVING

169	Calories
8 g	Fat (44.2% calories from fat)
5 g	Protein
19 g	Carbohydrate
2 g	Dietary Fiber
13 mg	Cholesterol
1212 mg	Sodium

SERVES 10 | DAIRY · FREEZES

Carrot Ginger Soup

2–3 large shallots, peeled and finely diced

1 Tbsp. | 15 mL olive oil

12 medium carrots (2 lbs. | 1 kg), peeled and thinly sliced

2½ Tbsp. | 40 mL fresh ginger, grated

1 tsp. | 5 mL salt

½ tsp. | 2 mL black pepper

6 cups | 1.5 L stock

1 Tbsp. | 15 mL lemon juice

1 Tbsp. | 15 mL honey

1 cup | 250 mL half-and-half

Ginger gives this soup a nice hit of heat. If you are not a huge ginger fan, cut the ginger down to 1 Tbsp. / 15 mL and try it that way.

METHOD

Sauté shallots in olive oil for 3–5 minutes over medium heat, until tender.

Add the carrots and ginger and sauté another minute.

Add the seasonings and stock, cover, set heat to high and bring to a boil. Reduce heat and simmer for 30 minutes.

Purée the soup. (See *Puréeing Soups* on page 9 in the Techniques section.)

Add the lemon juice, honey and half-and-half and return to the stove for a few minutes, until it's hot. Stir as it heats to avoid scorching.

PER SERVING

291	Calories
25 g	Fat (76.0% calories from fat)
3 g	Protein
15 g	Carbohydrate
2 g	Dietary Fiber
9 mg	Cholesterol
1144 mg	Sodium

SERVES 10 | DAIRY · FREEZES · PASSOVER

Celery Root Soup with Roasted Garlic

1 head garlic, left whole

1 small yellow onion, finely chopped

2 Tbsp. | 25 mL olive oil

1 medium red potato, peeled and sliced

1 large celery root (1 lb. | 500 g or nearly 2 lbs. | 1 kg before peeling), peeled and sliced ⅛ inch | 3 mm thick

4 cups | 1 L stock

2 tsp. | 10 mL salt

¼ tsp. | 1 mL black pepper

½ cup | 125 mL half-and-half

Roasted garlic adds a very subtle and sweet garlic flavor to soups. It works really well with cream soups and adds something special to the celery root.

METHOD

Preheat oven to 350°F (180°C). Wrap the head of garlic in aluminum foil, place in the oven and roast for approximately 45 minutes. Allow to cool, then peel.

Over medium heat, sauté onion in olive oil for 2–3 minutes. Add the potato, celery root, stock, salt, pepper and roasted garlic. Cover and bring to a boil. Simmer 25 minutes, or until the vegetables are tender.

Purée the soup. (See *Puréeing Soups* on page 9 in the Techniques section.)

Add the half-and-half, heat through and serve.

PER SERVING

197	Calories
12 g	Fat (51.2% calories from fat)
5 g	Protein
20 g	Carbohydrate
4 g	Dietary Fiber
11 mg	Cholesterol
2677 mg	Sodium

SERVES 4 | DAIRY · FREEZES · PASSOVER

White Soup

1 small white onion, peeled and chopped small

1 small leek, white part only, washed well and sliced thinly

2 Tbsp. | 25 mL olive oil

1–2 cloves garlic (1 tsp. | 5 mL), crushed

1 stalk celery, chopped small

1 small turnip, peeled and thinly sliced

2 small parsnips, peeled and thinly sliced

2 medium red potatoes, peeled and thinly sliced

3 sprigs fresh thyme (or ½ tsp. | 2 mL dried)

1 tsp. | 5 mL salt

¼ tsp. | 1 mL black pepper

5 cups | 1.25 L stock

½ cup | 125 mL half-and-half

This is a fantastic winter soup. Serve it garnished with croutons.

METHOD

Sauté onion and leek in olive oil over medium heat for 3–4 minutes.

Add garlic and sauté another 1–2 minutes.

Add the rest of the ingredients except the cream, cover and bring to a boil. Reduce heat to medium-low and simmer 20 minutes.

Pull out the thyme stems. Purée the soup. See *Puréeing Soups* on page 9 in the Techniques section.

Add the half-and-half and warm through.

PER SERVING

131	Calories
6 g	Fat (39.8% calories from fat)
3 g	Protein
17 g	Carbohydrate
2 g	Dietary Fiber
6 mg	Cholesterol
1219 mg	Sodium

SERVES 8 | DAIRY • FREEZES • PASSOVER

Sweet Potato Chowder

1 small yellow onion, peeled and cut into ½-inch | 1-cm cubes

1 stalk celery, cut into ½-inch | 1-cm cubes

2 Tbsp. | 25 mL olive oil

1 small carrot, peeled and cut into ½-inch | 1-cm cubes

1 large or 2 small sweet potatoes (1 lb. | 500 g), peeled and cut into ½-inch | 1-cm cubes

4 cups | 1 L stock

½ cup | 125 mL frozen corn kernels

½ small red pepper, cored, seeded and diced

2 tsp. | 10 mL salt

½ tsp. | 2 mL black pepper

3 Tbsp. | 75 mL all-purpose flour

1 cup | 250 mL half-and-half

This soup has lots of beautiful colors, flavors and textures. The sweet potatoes, red peppers and corn add a slight sweetness.

METHOD

Over medium-low heat, sauté onion and celery in olive oil for 5–7 minutes, until the onion is wilted.

Add carrot, sweet potato and stock, cover and bring to a boil over high heat. Reduce the temperature and simmer on medium-low for 10–12 minutes.

Add the corn, red pepper, salt and pepper and simmer another 10 minutes.

In a separate bowl, whisk together the flour and half-and-half, making sure to whisk out any lumps. Pour this mixture into the soup, stirring well to incorporate.

Let the soup simmer another 3–4 minutes, so the flour cooks and the soup thickens.

PER SERVING

166	Calories
8 g	Fat (41.0% calories from fat)
3 g	Protein
22 g	Carbohydrate
2 g	Dietary Fiber
11 mg	Cholesterol
1302 mg	Sodium

SERVES 8 | DAIRY · FREEZES

Sweet Potato Soup

4 medium shallots, peeled and chopped

2 Tbsp. | 25 mL olive oil

2 medium red potatoes, peeled and sliced
¼ inch | 5 mm thick

2–3 medium sweet potatoes, peeled and sliced
¼ inch | 5 mm thick

2 medium carrots, peeled and sliced ¼ inch | 5 mm thick

8–12 cloves garlic (2 Tbsp. | 25 mL), crushed

1 bay leaf

1 tsp. | 5 mL salt

¼ tsp. | 1 mL black pepper

6 cups | 1.5 L stock

½ cup | 125 mL half-and-half (optional)

This soup is a favorite with our restaurant customers. It's also the perfect beginning to a Thanksgiving or fall dinner. Leave the half-and-half out if you are using it for a starter with a meat meal.

METHOD

Over medium heat, sauté the shallots in olive oil 3–5 minutes, until they are wilted but have not started to brown.

Add potatoes, sweet potatoes, carrots, garlic, bay leaf, salt and pepper to the pot and sauté for another 1–2 minutes.

Add the stock, cover and bring to a boil over high heat. Reduce heat to medium-low and simmer, until all the vegetables are fork-tender, approximately 25 minutes. Remove the bay leaf from the pot.

Purée the soup. See *Puréeing Soups* on page 9 in the Techniques section. If you see that the soup is really loose as you go, leave some of the liquid out. If the soup is too thick add some extra stock or water. I like the consistency to be a little looser than baby food.

If you choose, you can now add the half-and-half and mix it in, or swirl it into each bowl as a garnish. This soup tastes great without it too, so if you want to leave it out, you can!

Check the soup for salt and pepper and serve!

PER SERVING

264	Calories
7 g	Fat (22.3% calories from fat)
7 g	Protein
46 g	Carbohydrate
5 g	Dietary Fiber
6 mg	Cholesterol
1214 mg	Sodium

SERVES 10 | DAIRY · FREEZES · PASSOVER

Potato Leek Soup

4–5 large leeks (1 lbs. | 500 g), white part only, washed and sliced

¼ cup | 50 mL olive oil

4 medium red potatoes (2 lbs. | 1 kg), peeled and cut into ½-inch | 1-cm cubes

1 tsp. | 5 mL salt

¼ tsp. | 1 mL pepper

4 cups | 1 L stock

6 Tbsp. | 90 mL all-purpose flour

1 cup | 250 mL half-and-half

2 cups | 500 mL 2% milk

Some people prefer this soup puréed and smooth, but I like it chunky. Others prefer it chilled, but I like it hot.

METHOD

Over medium heat, sauté leeks in olive oil until they have wilted and gone a little translucent, approximately 3–4 minutes. (Stir constantly so that none of the leeks burn.)

Add the potatoes, salt, pepper and stock, cover and bring to a boil. Reduce heat to medium-low, and simmer 15 minutes, until the potatoes are fork-tender.

In a bowl, whisk the flour, half-and-half and milk together. Make sure all the flour is whisked in well and there are no lumps, or your soup will have dumplings. Slowly pour this mixture into the simmering soup, stirring constantly.

Allow the soup to come to the boil again, and cook for one minute while stirring. This will allow the soup to thicken.

Check the soup for seasoning and serve.

PER SERVING

178	Calories
8 g	Fat (40.5% calories from fat)
5 g	Protein
22 g	Carbohydrate
2 g	Dietary Fiber
10 mg	Cholesterol
709 mg	Sodium

SERVES 10 | DAIRY · FREEZES · PASSOVER

❧❧❧ Baked Potato Soup

3–4 medium baking potatoes (2 lbs. | 1 kg), skin on

1 small shallot, peeled and diced very finely

1 tsp. | 5 mL salt

¼ tsp. | 1 mL black pepper

1 Tbsp. | 15 mL olive oil

4 cups | 1 L stock

1 cup | 250 mL half-and-half

¾ cup | 175 mL 2% milk

2 Tbsp. | 25 mL all-purpose flour

4 oz. | 125 mL grated cheddar cheese

3 Tbsp. | 45 mL light sour cream

3–4 large green onions (scallions), thinly sliced

Add any of your favorite potato toppings and enjoy this baked potato in soup form!

METHOD
Place well-washed, whole baking potatoes on baking sheet and bake for one hour and 15 minutes in a 350°F (180°C) oven. Set aside and cool enough to handle. Cut potatoes into 1-inch (2.5-cm) cubes.

Sauté shallot, salt and pepper in olive oil for 5–8 minutes over medium heat. Add stock, cover and bring to a boil. Reduce heat and simmer, covered, on medium-low for 10 minutes. Add potatoes and simmer another 10 minutes.

In a bowl, whisk together the half-and-half, milk and flour. Add this mixture to the soup, stirring as you pour it in. Bring soup back to a boil and allow to simmer 3–4 minutes.

Garnish each bowl of soup with grated cheddar cheese, sour cream and sliced green onion or any other potato toppings that you enjoy.

PER SERVING

237	Calories
11 g	Fat (41.5% calories from fat)
9 g	Protein
27 g	Carbohydrate
2 g	Dietary Fiber
28 mg	Cholesterol
1130 mg	Sodium

SERVES 8 | DAIRY · FREEZES

Butternut Squash Soup

2 medium butternut squash (2 lbs. | 1 kg), peeled, seeded and cubed

1 small yellow onion, peeled and coarsely chopped

¼ tsp. | 1 mL ground nutmeg

½ tsp. | 2 mL ground allspice

5 cups | 1.25 L stock

1 bay leaf

1 tsp. | 5 mL salt

¼ tsp. | 1 mL black pepper

½ cup | 125 mL half-and-half

Serve with croutons or toasted pecans as a garnish to add a great crunch to the soup. You can also leave the half-and-half out completely or substitute non-dairy creamer.

METHOD

Put the squash, onion, nutmeg, allspice, stock and bay leaf into a soup pot and bring to a boil over high heat. Reduce the heat and continue simmering on medium-low for approximately 20 minutes, until the squash is soft.

Remove the bay leaf and purée the soup. (See *Puréeing Soups* on page 9 in the Techniques section.)

Season with salt and pepper and add half-and-half. Heat through and serve.

PER SERVING

148	Calories
5 g	Fat (29.2% calories from fat)
4 g	Protein
23 g	Carbohydrate
3 g	Dietary Fiber
11 mg	Cholesterol
2407 mg	Sodium

SERVES 4 | DAIRY · FREEZES · PASSOVER

Roasted Acorn Squash Soup

2 medium acorn squash (1 lb. | 500 g each)

olive oil for brushing

1 cup | 250 mL water

2–3 medium shallots, peeled and sliced

2 Tbsp. | 25 mL olive oil

2–3 cloves garlic (1½ tsp. | 7 mL), crushed

1 tsp. | 5 mL fresh ginger, finely minced

¼ tsp. | 1 mL ground nutmeg

½ tsp. | 2 mL black pepper

1 tsp. | 5 mL salt

1 medium carrot, peeled and sliced

2 medium red potatoes, peeled and sliced

6 cups | 1.5 L stock

½ cup | 125 mL half-and-half (optional)

Butternut squash would be great here as well. The nutmeg and ginger are perfect matches for the squash.

METHOD

Wash the squash well and cut them in half, lengthwise. Brush a little olive oil on each of the cut sides and place the halves, cut-side down, on a baking sheet that has raised edges. I like to use parchment paper to keep it from sticking. Roast the squash in a 425°F (220°C) oven for half an hour, then turn the squash over, add the water, cover with aluminum foil and continue to cook for another 15 minutes. Pull the squash out of the oven, allow to cool until you feel comfortable handling them and peel.

Over medium heat, sauté the shallots in olive oil, until wilted, about 2–3 minutes, stirring constantly.

Continue stirring while adding the garlic, ginger and other spices. Sauté for another minute.

Add the carrot, potatoes, squash and stock, cover and bring to a boil. Reduce heat to low and simmer for 20 minutes, until all of the vegetables are fork-tender.

Purée the soup. See *Puréeing Soups* on page 9 in the Techniques sections. I like the consistency to be a little looser than baby food, but it's all about how *you* like it!

If you want to add the half-and-half do so, and mix it in. Or you can use it to garnish each bowl as you serve it. Or you can leave it out completely and it will still taste great!

Check the soup for salt and pepper and serve!

PER SERVING	
157	Calories
6 g	Fat (33.8% calories from fat)
4 g	Protein
23 g	Carbohydrate
2 g	Dietary Fiber
6 mg	Cholesterol
1397 mg	Sodium

SERVES 8 | DAIRY · FREEZES · PASSOVER

Easy Pumpkin Soup

1 small red onion, peeled and finely diced

2 Tbsp. | 25 mL olive oil

1 tsp. | 5 mL ground ginger

½ tsp. | 2 mL ground nutmeg

1½ tsp. | 7 mL salt

¼ tsp. | 1 mL black pepper

1 bay leaf

¼ tsp. | 1 mL ground allspice

1 tsp. | 5 mL granulated sugar

1 can (28 oz. | 796 mL) pumpkin

5 cups | 1.25 L stock

1 cup | 250 mL half-and-half

The easy part of this soup is the canned pumpkin. There is no peeling the hard skins away—no roasting —just open the can and add it to the soup.

METHOD

Over medium-low heat, sauté the onion in olive oil for 5–8 minutes, stirring occasionally, until wilted but not browned.

Add all of the seasonings and cook another 30 seconds.

Add the pumpkin and stock, making sure to blend the pumpkin in well. If you leave any chunks of pumpkin, you risk burning them. Cover and bring the soup to a boil over high heat. Reduce the temperature and simmer for 20 minutes.

Add the half-and-half, remove the bay leaf and serve.

PER SERVING

102	Calories
6 g	Fat (53.2% calories from fat)
2 g	Protein
10 g	Carbohydrate
3 g	Dietary Fiber
9 mg	Cholesterol
1076 mg	Sodium

SERVES 10 | DAIRY • FREEZES

Pumpkin Soup

2½ lbs. | 1.25 kg pumpkin flesh (3½ lbs. | 1.75 kg whole pumpkin)

3 small shallots, peeled and thinly sliced

1 Tbsp. | 15 mL olive oil

1 medium carrot, peeled and coarsely chopped

¼ tsp. | 1 mL ground nutmeg

1 bay leaf

½ tsp. | 2 mL ground ginger

2 tsp. | 10 mL salt

½ tsp. | 2 mL black pepper

5 cups | 1.25 L stock

1 cup | 250 mL half-and-half

1 Tbsp. | 15 mL fresh ginger, grated

Keep the seeds from the pumpkin, clean them well, toss them with salt and roast them in the oven to make a great garnish for this soup.

METHOD

Preheat oven to 400°F (200°C). Cut the pumpkin in half, clean and scoop out all of the seeds. Brush or spray the cut sides of the pumpkin with olive oil, and place cut-side down on a baking sheet (with parchment paper or aluminum foil) and roast for 25 minutes. Turn the pumpkin over and roast another 25 minutes. When the pumpkin has cooled enough to handle, scoop all of the meat from the skin. Discard skin.

In a soup pot, over medium heat, sauté shallots in olive oil for 3–4 minutes. Add the pumpkin, carrot and spices (except for the fresh ginger). Add the stock, cover and bring to a boil. Reduce heat and simmer for 35 minutes on medium-low.

Remove the bay leaf and purée the soup. See *Puréeing Soups* on page 9 in the Techniques section.

Add the half-and-half and the fresh ginger and return the soup to the stove to heat through, 1–3 minutes. (If the soup has cooled before puréeing, it will take longer to reheat.)

PER SERVING

121	Calories
6 g	Fat (42.1% calories from fat)
4 g	Protein
15 g	Carbohydrate
1 g	Dietary Fiber
11 mg	Cholesterol
1481 mg	Sodium

SERVES 8 | DAIRY · FREEZES

Curried Red Lentil Soup with Yogurt

2 Tbsp. | 25 mL olive oil

1 stalk celery, finely diced

1 small yellow onion, peeled and finely diced

1 small carrot, peeled and finely diced

1 large jalapeno pepper, seeded, cored and minced

1 tsp. | 5 mL ground cumin

¼ tsp. | 1 mL chili powder

¼ tsp. | 1 mL ground cardamom

¼ tsp. | 1 mL ground turmeric

⅛ tsp. | .5 mL ground nutmeg

¼ tsp. | 1 mL ground coriander

¼ tsp. | 1 mL ground ginger

1 tsp. | 5 mL curry powder, medium

1–2 cloves garlic (1 tsp. | 5 mL), crushed

1 tsp. | 5 mL salt

¼ tsp. | 1 mL black pepper

6 cups | 1.5 L stock

1 cup | 250 mL dried red lentils, picked through and well rinsed

½ cup | 125 mL low-fat yogurt

Lots of ingredients but very simple to put together. Dry spices lose their flavors as they sit, so buy them in small quantities and use them up! The cool, slightly tart flavor of the yogurt complements the complex mix of spices.

METHOD

Over medium-low heat, sauté the vegetables in olive oil for 10 minutes, until they are soft and beginning to brown.

Add all of the spices and cook for another minute, stirring constantly.

Add the stock and lentils, cover and bring to a boil over high heat. Reduce heat and simmer for 10 minutes—the lentils will break down and make a thick soup.

Garnish each bowl of soup with 1 Tbsp. (15 mL) of yogurt.

PER SERVING

166	Calories
5 g	Fat (27.3% calories from fat)
10 g	Protein
21 g	Carbohydrate
10 g	Dietary Fiber
2 mg	Cholesterol
1400 mg	Sodium

SERVES 8 | DAIRY • FREEZE WITHOUT YOGURT

Leek and Spinach Soup

2–3 medium leeks, sliced ¼ inch | 5 mm thick

¼ cup | 50 mL olive oil

4 cups | 1 L firmly packed spinach leaves (1 lb. | 500 g), cut in ½-inch | 1-cm strips

2–4 cloves garlic (2 tsp. | 10 mL), crushed

1½ tsp. | 7 mL salt

¼ tsp. | 1 mL black pepper

⅛ tsp. | .5 mL nutmeg

3 Tbsp. | 45 mL all-purpose flour

2 cups | 500 mL half-and-half

4 cups | 1 L 2% milk

⅓ cup | 75 mL Parmesan cheese, finely grated

This soup can be served as it is, or puréed. Top it with some crunchy croutons for a contrast of textures.

METHOD

Over medium-low heat, sauté leeks 4–5 minutes in olive oil. They should be wilted, but not browned.

Add the spinach and cook approximately 2 minutes.

Add the garlic and seasonings and sauté another minute. Then add the flour and cook 1 minute, stirring constantly.

Add the half-and-half and milk and bring the soup to a low boil. Simmer for 5–7 minutes, until the soup has thickened slightly.

Add the Parmesan cheese and stir it in, making sure to stir out any lumps.

PER SERVING

231	Calories
17 g	Fat (65.7% calories from fat)
8 g	Protein
12 g	Carbohydrate
trace	Dietary Fiber
34 mg	Cholesterol
545 mg	Sodium

SERVES 8 | DAIRY • DON'T FREEZE

Cream of Broccoli Soup

1 medium white onion, peeled and cut into ½-inch (1-cm) dice

3 Tbsp. | 45 mL olive oil

2 lbs. | 1 kg broccoli florets (stems optional), washed well and coarsely chopped

5 cups | 1.25 L stock

1½ cups | 375 mL half-and-half

5 Tbsp. | 70 mL all-purpose flour

1½ tsp. | 7 mL salt

½ tsp. | 2 mL black pepper

This soup would work well with asparagus, carrots, cauliflower or any preferred vegetable in place of the broccoli. You may need to adjust some of the cooking times, adding the half-and-half and flour mixture once the vegetables are tender. You can also purée any of these soups for a more elegant variation.

METHOD

Over medium-low heat, sweat the onion in olive oil for 5–8 minutes. The onion should be wilted, but not brown.

If you are using broccoli stems as well as florets, the stems need to be peeled before they are chopped up for the soup. Use a vegetable peeler or a paring knife to take the tough, fibrous skin from the tender flesh. Then chop up the stems. Reserve the florets for later.

Add the chopped broccoli stems, if using, and the stock. Cover and bring to a boil over high heat. Reduce to medium-low and simmer for 5 minutes.

Add the broccoli florets and simmer another 5 minutes.

In a separate bowl, whisk together the half-and-half and flour, making sure there are no lumps. Slowly whisk this mixture into the soup. Add the salt and pepper.

Allow the soup to simmer for another 2–3 minutes, until the flour is cooked and the soup has thickened.

PER SERVING

128	Calories
9 g	Fat (60.2% calories from fat)
5 g	Protein
9 g	Carbohydrate
3 g	Dietary Fiber
13 mg	Cholesterol
1101 mg	Sodium

SERVES 10 | DAIRY · FREEZES

❧ Cream of Mushroom Soup

2 medium shallots, peeled and finely chopped

¼ cup | 50 mL olive oil

1½ lbs. | 750 g button mushrooms, washed and sliced ¼ inch | 5 mm thick

1 cup | 250 mL white wine

2 cups | 500 mL stock

1½ tsp. | 7 mL salt

½ tsp. | 2 mL black pepper

1 cup | 250 mL 2% milk

1 cup | 250 mL half-and-half

6 Tbsp. | 90 mL all-purpose flour

Use whatever white wine you like to drink. If you don't like to drink it, don't use it! You can leave it out completely, but it adds a nice tanginess. Try replacing it with a squeeze of fresh lemon juice.

METHOD

Over medium-high heat, sauté the shallots in olive oil until just tender, but not browned, about 5 minutes.

Add the mushrooms and sauté another 5 minutes or until they start to release their juices.

Add the wine and cook another 2–3 minutes, allowing some of the alcohol to cook off.

Add the stock, salt and pepper and allow to simmer, covered, for 10–15 minutes.

Add the milk and bring to a boil. Mix the half-and-half and the flour together, ensuring that there are no lumps. Whisk the half-and-half and flour mixture into the soup and allow the soup to cook for 2–3 minutes. When the flour is cooked through, the soup will have thickened and will be ready to eat.

PER SERVING

192	Calories
11 g	Fat (57.0% calories from fat)
5 g	Protein
15 g	Carbohydrate
1 g	Dietary Fiber
13 mg	Cholesterol
805 mg	Sodium

SERVES 8 | DAIRY · FREEZES

Cream of Tomato Soup

1 small yellow onion, peeled and finely chopped

1 tsp. | 5 mL granulated sugar

2 Tbsp. | 25 mL olive oil

2–4 cloves garlic (2 tsp. | 10 mL), crushed

½ cup | 125 mL firmly packed fresh basil, cut into thin strips

1 tsp. | 5 mL salt

¼ tsp. | 1 mL black pepper

1 can (28 oz. | 796 mL) diced tomatoes

1 can (28 oz. | 796 mL) crushed tomatoes

3 cups | 750 mL stock

1½ cups | 375 mL heavy or whipping (35%) cream

This is my version of an old favorite. Tear open a bag of soda crackers, maybe make a grilled cheese sandwich, and enjoy.

I have tried making this soup with half-and-half and 2% milk and found that it curdled. Thirty-five percent cream (heavy or whipping) is the way to go. If freezing, do not add cream until after thawing.

METHOD

Over medium-low heat, sauté the onion and granulated sugar in olive oil for 5–8 minutes. The sugar will help draw out the juices from the onion and will start to caramelize. Don't brown the onions too much—you want them to soften and brown slightly.

Add the garlic and cook another 30 seconds, stirring constantly.

Add basil, salt, pepper, tomatoes and stock and cover the pot. Turn the heat up to bring the soup to a boil. Once it starts to boil, turn the heat back down so that the soup cooks at a gentle simmer. Cook on low for 20 minutes.

Purée the soup. See *Puréeing Soups* on page 9 in the Techniques section.

Add the cream and heat through.

PER SERVING

255	Calories
21 g	Fat (69.9% calories from fat)
4 g	Protein
16 g	Carbohydrate
3 g	Dietary Fiber
61 mg	Cholesterol
980 mg	Sodium

SERVES 8 | DAIRY · FREEZE WITHOUT WHIPPING CREAM · PASSOVER

Cream of Vegetable Soup

¼ lb. | 125 g button mushrooms, cleaned and quartered

1 small carrot, peeled and diced

2 cups | 500 mL cauliflower, cut into florets

1⅔ cups | 400 mL broccoli, cut into florets

1 stalk celery, cubed

1 small yellow onion, peeled and chopped

1 small zucchini, cubed

2 Tbsp. | 25 mL olive oil

6 cups | 1.5 L stock

1½ tsp. | 7 mL salt

¼ tsp. | 1 mL black pepper

1 cup | 250 mL 2% milk

1 cup | 250 mL half-and-half

6 Tbsp. | 90 mL all-purpose flour

Substitute any vegetables you like in this soup. You can also use frozen vegetables instead of the fresh, but you will need to adjust your cooking time, simmering just until the vegetables are tender before adding the milk.

METHOD

Place the mushrooms, carrot, cauliflower, broccoli, celery, onion, zucchini, olive oil, stock, salt and pepper in a soup pot. Cover and place over high heat and bring to a boil. Turn the heat down to medium-low and simmer for 25 minutes.

Add the 2% milk.

In a bowl, whisk together the half-and-half and flour. Make sure there are no lumps. Add this mixture to the soup pot, stirring constantly as you pour it in. Bring the soup back to a boil and cook 3–4 minutes. As the soup boils, the flour will thicken it.

PER SERVING

120	Calories
7 g	Fat (49.4% calories from fat)
4 g	Protein
12 g	Carbohydrate
2 g	Dietary Fiber
11 mg	Cholesterol
1251 mg	Sodium

SERVES 10 | DAIRY · FREEZES

Roasted Bell Pepper Soup

9 medium bell peppers (4 lbs. | 2 kg)

1 medium red onion, peeled and coarsely chopped

2 Tbsp. | 25 mL olive oil

2 medium red potatoes, peeled and coarsely chopped

6 cups | 1.5 L vegetable stock

1 tsp. | 5 mL salt

¼ tsp. | 1 mL black pepper

½ cup | 125 mL half-and-half

sour cream, chives or croutons for garnish

PER SERVING

277	Calories
8 g	Fat (26.3% calories from fat)
8 g	Protein
45 g	Carbohydrate
7 g	Dietary Fiber
7 mg	Cholesterol
1500 mg	Sodium

SERVES 8 | DAIRY · FREEZES · PASSOVER

This is an elegant soup. It's great for entertaining and can be done ahead and reheated right before serving. If you find the soup too thick, add a little more stock or water. I prefer to use the hand blender to purée the soup. If you do not have one, use a blender or food processor. Use red, yellow, orange, purple or a combination of any bell peppers. I don't use green peppers because I find they make the soup bitter, but if you are a green pepper fan, try it!

METHOD

Preheat oven to 400°F (200°). Cut peppers in half, discard the seeds and stem and wash thoroughly. Place peppers on a baking sheet lined with parchment paper or aluminum foil, and roast for approximately half an hour, until the skins are charred. Not all of the skin will char, but there should be large patches of brown. Remove peppers from oven and place in a bowl. Cover with plastic wrap and allow to stand for at least 20 minutes. When the peppers are cool enough to handle, carefully peel off all the skin. Do not rinse the peppers under water, because it will wash away a lot of the flavor.

Over medium heat, sauté the onion in olive oil until it begins to wilt, about 5 minutes.

Add the potatoes, peppers, stock, salt and pepper and cover. Bring to a boil over high heat. Reduce heat and simmer on medium-low until potatoes are fork-tender, approximately 15 minutes.

Purée the soup. See *Puréeing Soups* on page 9 in the Techniques section.

Once you have a smooth soup, add the half-and-half. Check soup for salt and pepper seasoning.

Garnish with some sour cream swirled in, chives or croutons.

Roasted Corn Chowder

8 cobs of fresh corn (1 lb. | 500 g)

vegetable spray

1 medium yellow onion, peeled and chopped

1 small carrot, peeled and chopped small

2 stalks celery, chopped small

3 Tbsp. | 45 mL olive oil

3 cups | 750 mL stock

2 medium red potatoes, peeled and diced small

1½ tsp. | 7 mL salt

½ tsp. | 2 mL black pepper

3 Tbsp. | 45 mL all-purpose flour

2½ cups | 625 mL 2% milk

1½ cups | 375 mL half-and-half

Roasting the corn brings out its natural sugars. If fresh corn is not available, thaw and sauté some frozen corn until it gets some color on it.

METHOD

Preheat oven to 450°F (230°C). Shuck 8 cobs of corn. Make sure to get all of the silk off and wash well. Place the corn on a baking tray that you have sprayed with vegetable spray and roast for approximately 20 minutes. Turn the corn every 8 minutes or so. The corn will be ready when it has started to brown slightly on all sides. Set the corn aside and allow it to cool. Use a sharp knife or a mandolin and carefully cut the kernels off the cob—as much as you can—and put aside.

Over medium-low heat, sauté the onion, carrot and celery in olive oil for 5–7 minutes, until they are soft and wilted, but not browned.

Add the stock and potatoes, salt and pepper and bring to a simmer. Cook for 10 minutes.

Add the corn and cook for another 5 minutes.

In a separate bowl, whisk together the flour, milk and half-and-half. Make sure the mixture is well combined and there are no lumps. Whisk this slurry into the chowder. Bring the soup back up to a simmer and allow the flour to cook for a few minutes. The chowder will thicken after 4–5 minutes and be ready to serve.

PER SERVING

216	Calories
10 g	Fat (40.7% calories from fat)
6 g	Protein
27 g	Carbohydrate
3 g	Dietary Fiber
18 mg	Cholesterol
825 mg	Sodium

SERVES 10 | DAIRY · FREEZES

Roasted Tomato Soup

20 medium Roma (Italian plum) tomatoes (4 lbs. | 2 kg), washed and quartered

1 large red onion, peeled and cubed

10 cloves garlic

2 Tbsp. | 25 mL fresh oregano, washed and dried

½ cup | 125 mL fresh basil (firmly packed)

1½ tsp. | 7 mL salt

½ tsp. | 2 mL black pepper

¼ cup | 50 mL olive oil

2 cups | 500 mL water

½ cup | 125 mL 2% milk

Sour cream is a great garnish. This soup would also be great with some crunchy, garlicky homemade croutons.

METHOD

Preheat oven to 400°F (200°C). In an ovenproof dish, toss the tomatoes, onion, garlic, herbs, salt, pepper and oil together and roast, uncovered, for 20 minutes.

Add the water and return to the oven for another 20 minutes.

Purée the soup. See *Puréeing Soups* on page 9 in the Techniques section. I don't bother to strain the soup because I enjoy a little bit of texture in it, but pouring the soup through a fine-mesh strainer will give you a more elegant soup.

Add the milk and return soup to the stove to heat through.

PER SERVING

131	Calories
8 g	Fat (49.6% calories from fat)
3 g	Protein
15 g	Carbohydrate
3 g	Dietary Fiber
1 mg	Cholesterol
430 mg	Sodium

SERVES 8 | DAIRY · FREEZES · PASSOVER

Chilled Avocado Soup

1 large yellow onion, peeled and coarsely chopped

1 whole jalapeno pepper, cored, seeded and coarsely chopped

¼ cup | 50 mL fresh lime juice

4 Haas avocados (1¼ lbs. | 625 g), peeled and pitted

2 cups | 500 mL low-fat yogurt

¼ cup | 50 mL half-and-half

1 tsp. | 5 mL salt

⅛ tsp. | .5 mL black pepper

2 medium Roma (Italian plum) tomatoes, seeded and finely diced

2 tsp. | 10 mL cilantro, chopped fine

A great soup to have on a hot summer day. Make it ahead and keep it in the refrigerator, covered well with plastic wrap.

METHOD

Coarsely chop the onion and jalapeno and purée in a food processor or blender.

Add the lime juice and purée again. Try to get this mixture as smooth as possible, then add the avocado and purée again. This soup base should have a smooth, creamy consistency.

Transfer to a bowl, stir in yogurt, half-and-half and season with salt and pepper, cover tightly with plastic wrap and refrigerate.

Just before serving, garnish with chopped tomatoes and cilantro.

PER SERVING

196	Calories
12 g	Fat (52.4% calories from fat)
7 g	Protein
18 g	Carbohydrate
3 g	Dietary Fiber
5 mg	Cholesterol
433 mg	Sodium

SERVES 6 | DAIRY • DON'T FREEZE

Chilled Potato and Watercress Soup

2 small leeks, white only, sliced thin

2 Tbsp. | 25 mL olive oil

3 medium red potatoes (1½ lbs. | 750 g), peeled and cubed

4 cups | 1 L stock

2 tsp. | 10 mL salt

½ tsp. | 2 mL black pepper

3 cups | 750 mL fresh watercress (firmly packed)

1 cup | 250 mL half-and-half

This is a great version of vichyssoise. I love it cold, but it's also good served hot. Try it and see which way you prefer it.

METHOD

Over medium-low heat, sauté the leeks in olive oil for 5 minutes, until they have wilted. Add the potatoes, stock, salt and pepper, cover and bring to a boil over high heat. Reduce the heat and simmer gently for 15–20 minutes, or until the potatoes are fork-tender.

Purée the soup. (See *Puréeing Soups* on page 9 in the Techniques section.)

Add the watercress and half-and-half and purée again. Try to get the soup as smooth as possible.

Transfer soup to a bowl, cover with a piece of wax paper and chill for at least 4 hours, or until cold.

PER SERVING

204	Calories
10 g	Fat (43.4% calories from fat)
5 g	Protein
25 g	Carbohydrate
2 g	Dietary Fiber
15 mg	Cholesterol
1730 mg	Sodium

SERVES 6 | DAIRY · DON'T FREEZE · PASSOVER

Chilled Roasted Beet Soup

6–8 small beets (1½ lbs. | 750 g), well scrubbed

½ cup | 125 mL cold water

1 Tbsp. | 15 mL balsamic vinegar

1 tsp. | 5 mL salt

¼ tsp. | 1 mL black pepper

1 cup | 250 mL half-and-half

A modern twist on a classic soup. Roasting the beets brings out the natural sugars and the balsamic vinegar replaces the sour salt usually found in borscht.

METHOD

Preheat oven to 350°F (180°C). Place beets on baking sheet lined with parchment paper, cover with aluminum foil and roast for 1½ hours, or until the beets are fork-tender. Allow the beets to cool enough so that you can handle them and peel.

Use a blender to purée the beets. Food processors and hand blenders can't purée the beets into a smooth enough texture. Add the water and continue to purée. Add the vinegar, salt, pepper and half-and-half and purée until the soup is as smooth as possible.

Transfer the soup to a bowl and chill for at least 4 hours.

PER SERVING

129	Calories
7 g	Fat (47.9% calories from fat)
4 g	Protein
14 g	Carbohydrate
3 g	Dietary Fiber
22 mg	Cholesterol
647 mg	Sodium

SERVES 4 | DAIRY • DON'T FREEZE • PASSOVER

Apple Cheddar Soup

2 small shallots, peeled and finely chopped

2 Tbsp. | 25 mL olive oil

1 tsp. | 5 mL ground cinnamon

½ tsp. | 2 mL salt

¼ tsp. | 1 mL black pepper

4–6 Granny Smith apples (1½ lbs. | 750 g), peeled, cored and sliced

3 cups | 750 mL stock

1 bay leaf

2 Tbsp. | 25 mL all-purpose flour

2 cups | 500 mL half-and-half

½ lb. | 250 g grated cheddar cheese

Like apple pie with a slice of cheddar cheese, this is a classic combination.

METHOD

Over medium-low heat, sauté the shallots in olive oil for 5–8 minutes, until the shallots are soft.

Add the cinnamon, salt and pepper and cook another 30 seconds.

Add the apples and sauté 3–4 minutes.

Add the stock and bay leaf, cover and bring the soup to a boil over high heat. Reduce the temperature and simmer the soup on medium-low for 10 minutes, or until the apples are soft.

Take out the bay leaf and purée the soup. See *Puréeing Soups* on page 9 in the Techniques section.

Return the soup to the stove and reheat if necessary.

In a separate bowl, whisk together the flour and half-and-half. Pour this mixture into the hot soup and whisk together. Allow the soup to return to a simmer and cook another 2 minutes.

Add the grated cheddar cheese and mix until all of the cheese melts and has been incorporated.

PER SERVING

261	Calories
19 g	Fat (64.6% calories from fat)
10 g	Protein
14 g	Carbohydrate
2 g	Dietary Fiber
50 mg	Cholesterol
813 mg	Sodium

SERVES 9 | DAIRY · DON'T FREEZE

Beer Cheese Soup

½ small yellow onion, peeled and finely chopped

1 small carrot, peeled and finely chopped

2 Tbsp. | 25 mL olive oil

3 cups | 750 mL beer

¼ cup | 50 mL all-purpose flour

1 cup | 250 mL 2% milk

1 cup | 250 mL half-and-half

1½ tsp. | 7 mL salt

¼ tsp. | 1 mL black pepper

1 lb. | 500 g grated cheddar cheese

1 cup | 250 mL air-popped popcorn, for garnish

Use whatever beer you like to drink. Using a light beer will make the flavor of the soup subtler than a dark beer. It's a rich soup, so go easy!

METHOD

Over medium-low heat, sweat the vegetables in olive oil for 12–15 minutes, until they are wilted but not brown.

Add the beer and bring it to a simmer. Allow the soup to simmer gently for 10 minutes.

In a separate bowl, whisk together the flour, milk and half-and-half. Whisk this mixture, along with the salt and pepper, into the soup and bring the soup back to a simmer. Cook for 3–5 minutes, allowing the flour to cook and the soup to thicken.

Using a whisk, add the cheese slowly to the soup, mixing well. Keep whisking until the cheese is completely incorporated.

Serve the soup with popcorn for a garnish and enjoy!

PER SERVING

374	Calories
26 g	Fat (67.1% calories from fat)
17 g	Protein
12 g	Carbohydrate
1 g	Dietary Fiber
73 mg	Cholesterol
787 mg	Sodium

SERVES 8 | DAIRY · FREEZES

Broccoli Cheddar Soup

1 small yellow onion, peeled and finely chopped

2 Tbsp. | 25 mL olive oil

1 lb. | 500 g broccoli florets (stems optional), cut in small pieces

1 tsp. | 5 mL salt

¼ tsp. | 1 mL black pepper

5 cups | 1.25 L stock

1 cup | 250 mL half-and-half

5 Tbsp. | 75 mL all-purpose flour

½ lb. | 250 g grated cheddar cheese

Broccoli and cheddar cheese are a wonderful combination. If you want to try something different, before you add the half-and-half and the flour, purée the soup and then continue as directed.

METHOD

Over medium-low heat, sweat the onion in olive oil for 5–8 minutes. Wilt the onion, but don't brown it.

If you are using broccoli stems as well as florets, peel them with a vegetable peeler or paring knife to remove the tough, fibrous skin from the tender flesh, then chop them up.

Add the broccoli, salt, pepper and stock to the soup pot, cover and bring to a boil over high heat. Turn the heat down so that the soup simmers on low and cook approximately 10 minutes. The broccoli should be tender but not overcooked.

In a separate bowl, whisk together the half-and-half and flour. Whisk this mixture into the soup and allow to simmer another 2–3 minutes, until the soup thickens.

Stir in the cheese until it is well incorporated and serve.

PER SERVING

315	Calories
23 g	Fat (64.3% calories from fat)
15 g	Protein
14 g	Carbohydrate
3 g	Dietary Fiber
55 mg	Cholesterol
1864 mg	Sodium

SERVES 6 | DAIRY • FREEZES

Cauliflower Cheddar Soup

1 small yellow onion, peeled and finely chopped

2 Tbsp. | 25 mL olive oil

1½ lbs. | 750 g cauliflower florets, cut in small pieces

1 tsp. | 5 mL salt

¼ tsp. | 1 mL black pepper

5 cups | 1.25 L stock

1 cup | 250 mL half-and-half

5 Tbsp. | 75 mL all-purpose flour

½ lb. | 250 g grated cheddar cheese

Cauliflower and cheddar are an amazing combination. Try puréeing the soup before adding the cheddar for a different texture.

METHOD

Over medium-low heat, sweat the onion in olive oil for 5–8 minutes. Wilt the onion, but don't brown it.

Add the cauliflower, salt, pepper and stock to the soup pot, cover and bring to a boil. Turn the heat down and simmer for approximately 10 minutes. The cauliflower should be tender, but not overcooked.

In a separate bowl, whisk together the half-and-half and flour. Whisk this mixture into the soup and allow to simmer another 2–3 minutes, until the soup thickens.

Stir in the cheese until it is well incorporated. Serve.

PER SERVING

322	Calories
23 g	Fat (62.7% calories from fat)
15 g	Protein
16 g	Carbohydrate
3 g	Dietary Fiber
55 mg	Cholesterol
1877 mg	Sodium

SERVES 6 | DAIRY · FREEZES

Cheddar Chowder

1 small yellow onion, peeled and coarsely chopped

1 small carrot, peeled and cut into ½-inch │ 1-cm cubes

2 stalks celery, coarsely chopped

¼ lb. │ 125 g button mushrooms, quartered

1 medium zucchini, cut into ½-inch │ 1-cm cubes

1 large or 2 small red potatoes, peeled and cut into ½-inch │ 1-cm cubes

1⅔ cups │ 400 mL broccoli florets, cut into small pieces

2 cups │ 500 mL cauliflower florets, cut into small pieces

2 Tbsp. │ 25 mL olive oil

6 cups │ 1.5 L stock

1 tsp. │ 5 mL salt

¼ tsp. │ 1 mL black pepper

2 cups │ 500 mL 2% milk

5 Tbsp. │ 75 mL all-purpose flour

1 lb. │ 500 g grated cheddar cheese

This was always a favorite of customers in our restaurant. A rich, cheesy soup with lots of chunky vegetables.

METHOD

Place all of the vegetables, olive oil, stock, salt and pepper into a soup pot. Place on high heat, covered, and bring to a boil. Reduce heat to medium-low and simmer for 20 minutes.

In a bowl, whisk together the milk and flour, making sure there are no lumps (unless you want dumplings!). Add this mixture to the soup, stirring as you pour.

Allow the soup to heat through again, 3–5 minutes. As it continues to heat, the flour will cook and the soup will thicken.

Add the shredded cheddar, stirring until it has completely melted and mixed into the soup.

Serve!

PER SERVING

310	Calories
20 g	Fat (56.1% calories from fat)
16 g	Protein
18 g	Carbohydrate
3 g	Dietary Fiber
51 mg	Cholesterol
1434 mg	Sodium

SERVES 10 │ DAIRY · FREEZES

Cheesy Potato Soup

1 medium yellow onion, peeled and finely chopped

2 Tbsp. | 25 mL olive oil

4 medium red potatoes (2 lbs. | 1 kg), skin on, washed and cut into ½-inch | 1-cm cubes

2 tsp. | 10 mL salt

¼ tsp. | 1 mL black pepper

6 cups | 1.5 L stock

1 cup | 250 mL half-and-half

¼ cup | 50 mL all-purpose flour

¾ lb. | 375 g grated cheddar cheese

Cheddar cheese and potatoes are a natural combination. The starch and dairy make it a perfect comfort food.

METHOD

Over medium-low heat, sauté onion in olive oil for 7–10 minutes, until it starts to lightly brown.

Add the potatoes, salt, pepper and stock, cover and bring to a boil. Simmer over low heat for half an hour, or until the potatoes are fork-tender.

In a separate bowl, whisk together the half-and-half and flour. Whisk this mixture into the soup and simmer another 2–3 minutes, until the soup has thickened.

Add the cheese and stir the soup until all of the cheese has melted and is well incorporated. Serve!

PER SERVING

368	Calories
22 g	Fat (53.2% calories from fat)
15 g	Protein
28 g	Carbohydrate
2 g	Dietary Fiber
56 mg	Cholesterol
1929 mg	Sodium

SERVES 8 | DAIRY · FREEZES

Chilled Avocado Soup | *page 88*

Summer Vegetable Soup with Pesto | *page 100*

Smoked Salmon and Dill Cream Soup | *page 106*

Saffron and Garlic Fish Soup | *page 105*

Chili Cheese Soup

1 small yellow onion, peeled and finely chopped

2 Tbsp. | 25 mL olive oil

4–6 cloves garlic (1 Tbsp. | 15 mL), crushed

1 whole jalapeno, cored, seeded and finely minced

1 Tbsp. | 15 mL chili powder

2 tsp. | 10 mL ground coriander

1 Tbsp. | 15 mL ground cumin

2 tsp. | 10 mL salt

½ tsp. | 2 mL black pepper

1 Tbsp. | 15 mL tomato paste

1 can (28 oz. | 796 mL) diced tomatoes

5 cups | 1.25 L water

1 can (16 oz. or 19 oz. | 540 mL) black beans, rinsed and drained

6 Tbsp. | 90 mL all-purpose flour

1 cup | 250 mL half-and-half

½ lb. | 250 g grated cheddar cheese

Serve this soup with taco chips and forget about the "no dunking" rules!

METHOD

Over medium-low heat, sauté the onion in olive oil for 7–10 minutes until wilted and just starting to brown.

Add garlic, jalapeno and all of the spices and sauté for 1 minute, stirring constantly.

Add tomato paste, diced tomatoes and water. Cover, bring to a gentle simmer and cook for half an hour.

Add the beans and continue to simmer for another half an hour.

In a separate bowl, whisk together the flour and half-and-half, making sure to get out all the lumps. Slowly pour this mixture into the soup, stirring as you pour so the mixture gets well incorporated right away. Allow to simmer another 2–3 minutes, until the flour is cooked and the soup thickens.

Add the cheddar cheese and mix well, allowing the cheese to melt. Enjoy!

PER SERVING

315	Calories
19 g	Fat (52.8% calories from fat)
15 g	Protein
23 g	Carbohydrate
6 g	Dietary Fiber
45 mg	Cholesterol
992 mg	Sodium

SERVES 8 | DAIRY · FREEZES

Mushroom Cheddar Chowder

1½ lbs. | 750 g button mushrooms, shredded

1 medium yellow onion, peeled and shredded

3 Tbsp. | 45 mL olive oil

1 tsp. | 5 mL salt

¼ tsp. | 1 mL black pepper

3 Tbsp. | 45 mL all-purpose flour

2 cups | 500 mL stock

2 cups | 500 mL 2% milk

1 cup | 250 mL sour cream

½ lb. | 250 g grated cheddar cheese

extra sour cream, cheddar cheese and chives for garnish

This is a simple and delicious recipe. In less than an hour, you will have a rich, filling and tasty soup. I use a food processor to shred the vegetables, but a box grater would work, or for a more rustic soup, use a knife and chop them a little larger. For a more elegant soup, before adding the sour cream and cheese, purée in a blender or food processor.

METHOD

Sauté mushrooms and onion in olive oil with salt and pepper over medium-high heat for 5–8 minutes, until they are soft and have released their natural juices. Do not let the juices evaporate or brown the vegetables.

Add the flour and cook for one minute, being sure to stir all the flour into the liquid.

Add stock and milk. Bring to a boil and allow to cook for 3–4 minutes while stirring.

Take the soup off the heat and add sour cream and cheese, making sure to thoroughly incorporate them.

Serve immediately or refrigerate and reheat later. When reheating, I recommend using a microwave or double boiler to avoid scorching.

Garnish with a dollop of sour cream, shredded cheddar and chopped chives.

PER SERVING

258	Calories
18 g	Fat (62.6% calories from fat)
10 g	Protein
14 g	Carbohydrate
2 g	Dietary Fiber
38 mg	Cholesterol
718 mg	Sodium

SERVES 10 | DAIRY · FREEZES

Onion and Swiss Cheese Soup

2 small leeks, cleaned well and sliced into thin rounds

5 medium onions, peeled and thinly sliced

2–3 medium shallots, peeled and thinly sliced

¼ cup | 50 mL olive oil

1 cup | 250 mL dry white wine

2 tsp. | 10 mL salt

½ tsp. | 2 mL black pepper

6 Tbsp. | 90 mL all-purpose flour

1 cup | 250 mL half-and-half

3 cups | 750 mL 2% milk

½ lb. | 250 g grated Swiss cheese

The 5 onions can be made up of any onions you like. I use mix of white, yellow and red onions. This soup is incredibly rich, so start with small portions.

METHOD

Over medium-low heat, sauté the leeks, onions and shallots in olive oil. Keep stirring the mixture and cook for approximately 50 minutes. It may seem like a long time but the onions need to cook slowly on low heat. Turn the heat up to medium-high and continue to cook for 10 minutes. The onions will caramelize slightly and take on a light brown color.

Add the white wine, salt and pepper. Allow the wine to evaporate completely, cooking another 10 minutes.

Add the flour and mix well into the onions, trying to get out any lumps. Cook 2–3 minutes.

Add the half-and-half and milk, bring to a boil and simmer 5 minutes.

Add the shredded Swiss cheese and stir until all the cheese has melted and is well incorporated.

PER SERVING

286	Calories
16 g Fat	(52.4% calories from fat)
12 g	Protein
21 g	Carbohydrate
2 g	Dietary Fiber
35 mg	Cholesterol
539 mg	Sodium

SERVES 10 | DAIRY · FREEZES

Summer Vegetable Soup with Pesto

Pesto

2 cups | 500 mL fresh basil leaves (firmly packed)

1–2 cloves garlic (1 tsp. | 5 mL), crushed

2 Tbsp. | 25 mL pine nuts, toasted

½ tsp. | 2 mL salt

¼ tsp. | 1 mL black pepper

5 Tbsp. | 75 mL olive oil

2 Tbsp. | 25 mL grated Parmesan cheese

Soup

6 cups | 1.5 L stock

½ small yellow onion, peeled and sliced into thin strips

1 small carrot, peeled, cut in half lengthwise and sliced into ¼-inch | 5-mm half-circles

5–6 small new potatoes, skin on, cut in half and sliced into ¼-inch | 5-mm half-circles

¼ lb. | 125 g button mushrooms, cut into ¼-inch | 5-mm slices

¼ cup | 50 mL green beans, tips cut off, then cut on diagonal into ½-inch | 1-cm pieces

3–4 spears asparagus, cut on diagonal into ½-inch | 1-cm pieces

½ tsp. | 2 mL salt

⅛ tsp. | .5 mL black pepper

1 small zucchini, cut in half lengthwise and sliced into ¼-inch | 5-mm half-circles

1 cup | 250 mL firmly packed spinach leaves (2 oz. | 50 g), cut into thin strips

The soup itself is light on flavor—but serve bowls up with a dollop of the pesto on top and you'll be amazed. You can add any vegetables you like—see what your garden has to offer.

METHOD

For the pesto, place the basil, garlic, pine nuts, salt and pepper in the bowl of a food processor. Purée for 30 seconds and then scrape down the sides. With the machine running, slowly pour in the olive oil and keep puréeing until you have a nice paste—don't worry if it's not liquefied, you want to see a few small pieces of basil and garlic. Scrape this mixture into a bowl and mix in the Parmesan cheese. Cover and refrigerate.

For the soup, bring the stock to a boil in a covered pot over high heat. Add onion, carrot, potatoes, mushrooms, green beans, asparagus and salt and pepper—reduce heat and simmer gently for 7 minutes.

Add the zucchini and spinach and simmer another 5 minutes.

Serve each bowl of soup with a large spoonful of pesto.

PER SERVING

189	Calories
15 g	Fat (67.0% calories from fat)
5 g	Protein
11 g	Carbohydrate
2 g	Dietary Fiber
1 mg	Cholesterol
1884 mg	Sodium

SERVES 6 | DAIRY · DON'T FREEZE

Tortellini Soup

½ small yellow onion, peeled and cut into ⅓-inch | 8-mm dice

1 Tbsp. | 15 mL olive oil

¼ lb. | 125 g mushrooms, cut into ⅓-inch | 8-mm dice

1–2 cloves garlic (1 tsp. | 5 mL), crushed

5 cups | 1.25 L stock

2 cups | 500 mL crushed tomatoes

1 tsp. | 5 mL salt

¼ tsp. | 1 mL black pepper

1 medium zucchini, cut into ⅓-inch | 8-mm dice

12 oz. | 375 g cheese tortellini

½ cup | 125 mL fresh basil (firmly packed), thinly sliced

3 Tbsp. | 45 mL Parmesan cheese

Great frozen tortellini is available these days, but if you have homemade, by all means, use it.

METHOD

Over medium-low heat, sauté onion in olive oil for 5–8 minutes, until soft.

Add mushrooms and sauté 5 minutes, or until they release their juices.

Add garlic and cook 30 seconds, stirring constantly.

Add stock and crushed tomatoes and bring to a boil, covered, over high heat. Reduce heat and simmer for 7–8 minutes.

Add the salt, pepper, zucchini and tortellini and cook approximately 8–12 minutes, or until the pasta is done. (Follow the tortellini package directions for cooking time. Fresh tortellini will take less time to cook, and should be added about 4 minutes after the zucchini.)

Add fresh basil just before serving. Garnish each bowl with a teaspoon (5 mL) of Parmesan cheese.

PER SERVING

184	Calories
6 g	Fat (27.0% calories from fat)
10 g	Protein
25 g	Carbohydrate
3 g	Dietary Fiber
30 mg	Cholesterol
1475 mg	Sodium

SERVES 8 | DAIRY • DON'T FREEZE

Fish Soups

❧ Cod Chowder

1 small yellow onion, peeled and coarsely chopped

2 Tbsp. | 25 mL olive oil

4 cups | 1 L stock

1 stalk celery, cut into ½-inch | 1-cm cubes

1 small carrot, peeled and cut into ½-inch | 1-cm cubes

2 medium red potatoes, peeled and cut into
½-inch | 1-cm cubes

1½ tsp. | 7 mL salt

½ tsp. | 2 mL black pepper

1 bay leaf

1 tsp. | 5 mL fresh sage, chopped (or ¼ tsp. | 1 mL dried)

3 Tbsp. | 45 mL all-purpose flour

1 cup | 250 mL half-and-half

1 lb. | 500 g cod fillet, cut into large chunks

You can substitute any firm-fleshed white fish for this chowder. I love the flavor the sage adds, but if you're not a sage fan, substitute fresh parsley—just hold off adding the parsley until serving.

METHOD

Sauté onion over medium-high heat in olive oil for 5–7 minutes.

Add stock, celery, carrot, potatoes, salt, pepper, bay leaf and sage and cover. Bring the soup to a boil, then turn down and simmer gently for 10–15 minutes, until the vegetables are just tender.

In a separate bowl, whisk together the flour and half-and-half, making sure to get out any lumps. Add this mixture to the soup, mixing it in well. Allow to simmer for 1–2 minutes, letting the flour cook.

Add the cod and cook for 3–5 minutes, or until the fish is just cooked.

Remove the bay leaf before serving.

PER SERVING

252	Calories
11 g	Fat (37.8% calories from fat)
18 g	Protein
21 g	Carbohydrate
2 g	Dietary Fiber
47 mg	Cholesterol
1599 mg	Sodium

SERVES 6 | FISH · DAIRY · DON'T FREEZE

Saffron and Garlic Fish Soup

5 cups | 1.25 L stock

⅛ tsp. | .5 mL saffron threads

2–3 cloves garlic (1½ tsp. | 7 mL), crushed

½ small red onion, peeled and diced

¼ small fennel bulb, cut into ⅓-inch | 8-mm cubes

½ medium red pepper, cored, seeded and cut into ⅓-inch | 8-mm cubes

1 small zucchini, cut into ⅓-inch | 8-mm cubes

1 tsp. | 5 mL salt

¼ tsp. | 1 mL black pepper

2 medium Roma (Italian plum) tomatoes, seeded and cut into ⅓-inch | 8-mm cubes

½ lb. | 250 g cod fillets, cut into large chunks

½ lb. | 250 g haddock fillets, cut into large chunks

This light broth with chunks of yellow fish and bites of vegetables gets its incredible color from saffron.

METHOD

Over high heat, bring stock and saffron to a boil in a covered soup pot. Add the garlic, onion, fennel and red pepper. Reduce heat and simmer, covered, for 5 minutes on medium-low.

Add the zucchini, salt, pepper, tomatoes and fish and simmer another 3–4 minutes, just long enough to cook the fish.

PER SERVING

99	Calories
2 g	Fat (14.6% calories from fat)
16 g	Protein
5 g	Carbohydrate
1 g	Dietary Fiber
38 mg	Cholesterol
1644 mg	Sodium

SERVES 6 | FISH · DON'T FREEZE · PASSOVER

Smoked Salmon and Dill Cream Soup

1 small red onion, peeled and coarsely chopped

2 Tbsp. | 25 mL olive oil

4 cups | 1 L 2% milk

2 Tbsp. | 25 mL all-purpose flour

1 cup | 250 mL half-and-half

2 Tbsp. | 25 mL cream cheese

6 oz. | 175 g smoked salmon slices (chop 1 oz. | 25 g into small dice and set aside for garnish)

2 Tbsp. | 25 mL fresh dill, finely chopped (1 Tbsp. | 15 mL set aside for garnish)

If you love a bagel smeared with cream cheese and lox, try this soup!

METHOD

Over medium-low heat, sauté onions in olive oil for 5–8 minutes, or until the onions are soft.

Add the 2% milk, cover and bring to a boil. Reduce heat and simmer for 5 minutes.

In a small bowl, whisk together flour and half-and-half. Add this mixture to the soup and whisk until completely blended. Cook another 2 minutes, allowing the flour to cook.

Remove the soup from the heat and add cream cheese, 5 oz. (150 g) of smoked salmon and 1 Tbsp. (15 mL) dill.

Purée the soup. See *Puréeing Soups* on page 9 in the Techniques section.

Pour soup into bowls and garnish with reserved smoked salmon and dill.

PER SERVING

242	Calories
15 g	Fat (56.5% calories from fat)
13 g	Protein
14 g	Carbohydrate
1 g	Dietary Fiber
39 mg	Cholesterol
335 mg	Sodium

SERVES 6 | FISH · DAIRY · DON'T FREEZE

Soupe de Poisson au Provence

¼ small red onion, peeled and cut into strips

1 small leek, white part only, sliced into
¼-inch | 5-mm strips

2 Tbsp. | 25 mL olive oil

¼ small fennel bulb, sliced into ¼-inch | 5-mm strips

¼ small red bell pepper, cored, seeded and cut into
¼-inch | 5-mm strips

1 tsp. | 5 mL herb de Provence

1 clove garlic (½ tsp. | 2 mL), crushed

½ tsp. | 2 mL salt

¼ tsp. | 1 mL black pepper

4 cups | 1 L stock

¼ cup | 50 mL low-sodium tomato juice

½ lb. | 250 g haddock fillets, cut into large chunks

2 small Roma (Italian plum) tomatoes (¼ lb. | 125 g),
peeled, seeded and cut into strips

Herb de Provence is an herb combination used in the Provençal region of France. It is a mixture of rosemary, marjoram, thyme, basil, sage and lavender. You can find it already mixed in most supermarkets.

METHOD

Over low heat, sauté onion and leek in olive oil for 1–2 minutes.

Add the fennel, red pepper and seasonings and sauté another 1–2 minutes.

Add the stock and tomato juice, cover and bring to a boil over high heat. Reduce the temperature and simmer for 2–3 minutes.

Add the haddock and tomatoes and simmer another 3–5 minutes, until the fish is just done. When you cut into the fish there should be no translucency, but be careful not to overcook it.

PER SERVING

149	Calories
8 g	Fat (50.7% calories from fat)
13 g	Protein
6 g	Carbohydrate
1 g	Dietary Fiber
32 mg	Cholesterol
1799 mg	Sodium

SERVES 4 | FISH · DON'T FREEZE · PASSOVER

Meat Soups

Chicken Soup / Stock

4-lb. | 2-kg soup chicken

2 lbs. | 1 kg chicken bones

18 cups | 4.5 L cold water

3 whole carrots, peeled and chunked

3 whole celery stalks, chunked

2 whole onions, peeled, left whole

1 whole parsnip, peeled and chunked

salt, to taste

PER SERVING

37	Calories
trace	Fat (3.6% calories from fat)
1 g	Protein
9 g	Carbohydrate
2 g	Dietary Fiber
0 mg	Cholesterol
34 mg	Sodium

SERVES 10 | MEAT • FREEZES • PASSOVER

You need to use a soup chicken for this—an older chicken, sometimes called a boiling chicken or fowl. It will be much tougher than a chicken you would use to roast and eat, but the flavor it imparts to the soup will be much better.

If you are using kosher chicken, which is salted in the koshering process, don't salt the soup until you've tasted it, at the end.

When the soup is done, you can strain it for a beautiful, clear chicken stock, but I like to eat the vegetables that have absorbed so much great flavor. If you are using bones, though, you may wish to strain everything out, then add some fresh vegetables and simmer until they are fork-tender.

METHOD

Place the chicken, bones and cold water in a soup pot over high heat. As the soup begins to boil reduce the heat to medium-low. The chicken will release some scum, so keep an eye on the soup and skim off all the scum and foam until the liquid is clear. This may take up to an hour.

Add the vegetables and simmer for approximately 1½ hours, with the pot covered, leaving just a crack uncovered, allowing a little steam to escape. This will reduce the soup and the end result will be richer.

If you plan to use some of the chicken from the soup later on, as soon as the chicken is cooked, about 45 minutes, you can pull the chicken off the bones. Then return the bones to the soup. Most of the flavor in a chicken soup comes from the bones. For a stronger soup, don't bother with the whole chicken at all, just use 4–6 pounds (2–3 kg) of bones.

Chicken Soup with Fresh Herbs #1

¼ lb. | 125 g egg noodles

6 cups | 1.5 L chicken stock

2 Tbsp. | 25 mL fresh parsley, chopped fine

2 Tbsp. | 25 mL fresh dill, chopped fine

2 Tbsp. | 25 mL fresh chives, chopped fine

This is a great way to dress up homemade chicken stock when you want something a little different. When I have stock left over, I throw it in the freezer. Later, I thaw, heat and toss in some fresh herbs for a new take on the old, but great, standard.

METHOD

Cook the noodles according to package instructions.

Bring the chicken stock to a boil over high heat.

Add herbs and allow to simmer for 1 minute.

Add cooked and drained egg noodles and serve.

PER SERVING

111	Calories
2 g	Fat (18.1% calories from fat)
8 g	Protein
14 g	Carbohydrate
1 g	Dietary Fiber
18 mg	Cholesterol
768 mg	Sodium

SERVES 6 | MEAT · DON'T FREEZE

Chicken Soup with Fresh Herbs #2

¼ lb. | 125 g egg noodles

6 cups | 1.5 L chicken stock

1 Tbsp. | 15 mL fresh oregano, chopped fine

2 Tbsp. | 25 mL fresh basil, chopped fine

2 Tbsp. | 25 mL fresh parsley, chopped fine

Adding these herbs gives my homemade chicken stock a bit of an Italian flavor. It's also great if you substitute some cooked white rice for the egg noodles.

METHOD

Cook the noodles according to package instructions.

Bring the chicken stock to a boil over high heat. Add herbs and allow to simmer for 1 minute.

Add cooked and drained egg noodles and serve.

PER SERVING

111	Calories
2 g	Fat (18.1% calories from fat)
8 g	Protein
15 g	Carbohydrate
1 g	Dietary Fiber
18 mg	Cholesterol
768 mg	Sodium

SERVES 6 | MEAT · DON'T FREEZE

Asian Chicken Noodle Soup Bowl

1 Tbsp. | 15 mL canola oil

2 Tbsp. | 25 mL sesame oil

12 oz. | 375 g boned and skinned chicken breast, cut into thin strips

1 small carrot, sliced ⅛ inch | 3 mm thick

½ small red onion, peeled and cut into small chunks

2 cups | 500 mL cauliflower, cut into bite-sized pieces

6 oz. | 175 g button mushrooms, sliced ¼ inch | 5 mm thick

1⅔ cups | 400 mL broccoli florets, cut into bite-sized pieces

¼ small red and yellow bell pepper, cored, seeded and cut into ¼-inch | 5-mm strips

1 baby bok choy, sliced ⅓ inch | 8 mm thick

1 small zucchini, sliced into ¼-inch | 5-mm rounds

6–9 cloves garlic (1½ Tbsp. | 20 mL), crushed

1 Tbsp. | 15 mL fresh ginger, finely grated

4 Tbsp. | 60 mL soy sauce

1 cup | 250 mL snow peas, trimmed and tipped

2 cups | 500 mL bean sprouts

¾ cup | 175 mL canned water chestnuts, rinsed, drained and sliced

½ lb. | 250 g noodles (vermicelli), follow package directions

8 cups | 2 L hot chicken stock

3–4 green onions (scallions), sliced thin

No substitutes!! Use real chicken stock! It makes all the difference. I use vermicelli noodles, but rice noodles would be great. This hearty soup will serve 6 as a main course, 12 as a starter. It is best fresh, as reheating will make the vegetables mushy.

METHOD

Heat a large soup pot over medium heat for 1–2 minutes. Add both the canola and sesame oils then add the chicken. Cook for one minute, stirring constantly, then add each of the following ingredients, one at a time, waiting one minute between each addition: carrot, onion, cauliflower, mushrooms, broccoli, peppers, bok choy and zucchini.

After another minute, add the garlic and ginger, cook for 30 seconds and then add the soy sauce. Cook another minute, add the snow peas, bean sprouts and water chestnuts and cook another 1–2 minutes.

Add the cooked noodles. Toss the noodles so they are well coated and incorporated, then add the heated chicken stock. Let everything simmer for 1–2 minutes and serve!

PER SERVING

242	Calories
10 g	Fat (35.8% calories from fat)
24 g	Protein
16 g	Carbohydrate
5 g	Dietary Fiber
33 mg	Cholesterol
1095 mg	Sodium

SERVES 6 | MEAT · DON'T FREEZE

Chicken Cacciatore Soup

3 Tbsp. | 45 mL all-purpose flour

1¾ tsp. | 9 mL salt

⅝ tsp. | 3 mL black pepper

½ lb. | 250 g boneless, skinless chicken breast, cut into 1-inch | 2.5-cm cubes

¼ cup | 50 mL olive oil

1 small yellow onion, peeled and finely chopped

1 small carrot, peeled and sliced ⅛ inch | 3 mm thick

1 large zucchini, sliced ¼ inch | 5 mm thick

1 stalk celery, sliced ⅛ inch | 3 mm thick

¼ lb. | 125 g mushrooms, sliced ½ inch | 5 mm thick

½ large red bell pepper, seeded and cut into ⅓-inch | 8-mm dice

8–12 cloves garlic (2 Tbsp. | 25 mL), crushed

1½ tsp. | 7 mL dried oregano

1½ tsp. | 7 mL dried basil

¼ tsp. | 1 mL chili powder

1½ Tbsp. | 20 mL granulated sugar

2 Tbsp. | 25 mL tomato paste

1 can (28 oz. | 796 mL) diced tomatoes

4 cups | 1 L water

¾ cup | 175 mL dry macaroni

Don't overcook the chicken, or it will get tough. If you prefer to use dark meat, or a combination, go ahead.

METHOD

Mix the flour, ¼ tsp. (1 mL) of salt and ⅛ tsp. (.5 mL) of black pepper together. Dredge the chicken parts in the flour mixture, shaking off any excess. Using 2 Tbsp. (25 mL) of the olive oil, sauté the chicken pieces, sealing all sides, approximately 1 minute on each side. Place the chicken pieces on a paper towel to drain and set aside.

In a soup pot, sauté the vegetables in remaining 2 Tbsp. (25 mL) of olive oil over medium heat for 10 minutes.

Add the garlic, oregano, basil, chili powder, sugar and the remaining salt and black pepper. Cook for another minute.

Add the tomato paste and mix into the vegetables well, cooking for another minute.

Add the diced tomatoes and water, cover and bring to a boil. Simmer gently for 20 minutes over low heat.

Add the reserved chicken and pasta and continue simmering until the pasta is tender and the chicken is fully cooked, approximately 10 minutes.

PER SERVING

154	Calories
6 g	Fat (34.3% calories from fat)
7 g	Protein
19 g	Carbohydrate
3 g	Dietary Fiber
11 mg	Cholesterol
861 mg	Sodium

SERVES 10 | MEAT • FREEZES

Chicken Gumbo Soup

1 small yellow onion, peeled and finely chopped

1 small green pepper, seeded and chopped into
⅛-inch | 8-mm pieces

1 whole jalapeno, seeded and finely chopped

3 stalks celery, finely chopped

2 cups | 500 mL okra, washed, trimmed and cut into
3–4 pieces

1½ tsp. | 7 mL salt

¼ tsp. | 1 mL black pepper

¼ tsp. | 1 mL chili powder

1–2 cloves garlic (1 tsp. | 5 mL), crushed

¼ cup | 50 mL olive oil

¼ cup | 50 mL all-purpose flour

3 Tbsp. | 45 mL tomato paste

1 can (28 oz. | 796 mL) diced tomatoes

8 cups | 2 L stock

1 cup | 250 mL rice

½ lb. | 250 g cooked chicken, cut into
½ -inch | 1-cm cubes

I use fresh okra in this recipe, but if you can't find it, you can use frozen. Don't be alarmed by the somewhat slimy juices okra gives off. All the sliminess will disappear as it cooks.

METHOD

Over medium heat, sauté the onion, pepper, jalapeno, celery, okra, salt, pepper, chili powder and garlic in olive oil for 5–7 minutes. The vegetables should wilt, but not brown.

Add the flour and cook for 2–3 minutes, stirring constantly.

Add the tomato paste, diced tomatoes and stock. Cover and bring to a boil, then reduce the heat to medium-low and simmer for 25 minutes.

Add the rice and simmer for another 15 minutes.

Add the cooked chicken, and simmer until the chicken is heated through and the rice is tender.

PER SERVING

187	Calories
6 g	Fat (30.7% calories from fat)
10 g	Protein
23 g	Carbohydrate
2 g	Dietary Fiber
16 mg	Cholesterol
1415 mg	Sodium

SERVES 12 | MEAT · FREEZES

Chicken Satay Soup

1 small yellow onion, finely diced

2 Tbsp. | 25 mL olive oil

1–2 cloves garlic (1 tsp. | 5 mL), crushed

1 cup | 250 mL smooth peanut butter

5 cups | 1.25 L stock

½ lb. | 250 g skinless, boneless chicken breast, sliced
⅛ inch | 3 mm thick

1 cup | 250 mL bean sprouts

¼ cup | 50 mL canned water chestnuts, chopped into
small pieces

2 Tbsp. | 25 mL hot sauce

½ tsp. | 2 mL black pepper

3 Tbsp. | 45 mL soy sauce

2 Tbsp. | 25 mL fresh lime juice

1–2 medium green onions (scallions), thinly sliced

⅓ cup | 75 mL raw, unsalted peanuts, coarsely chopped

This soup is rich. I suggest serving it as a starter rather than a whole meal. To cut back on the richness, try the recipe with half the peanut butter. It won't have as much of a peanutty flavor, but it will be lighter and still full of great tastes.

METHOD

Over medium-low heat, sauté the onion in olive oil for 5–7 minutes, until wilted.

Add the garlic and sauté another half minute.

Add the peanut butter and stock and whisk together, making sure to incorporate all of the peanut butter into the liquid. Cover, bring to a boil, and simmer over low heat for 5 minutes.

Add the chicken breast and cook for 2–3 minutes, until the chicken is slightly underdone.

Add the bean sprouts, water chestnuts, hot sauce, black pepper and soy sauce and heat through.

Add lime juice.

Garnish the soup with chopped green onion and peanuts and serve.

PER SERVING

432	Calories
33 g	Fat (64.4% calories from fat)
24 g	Protein
16 g	Carbohydrate
4 g	Dietary Fiber
22 mg	Cholesterol
2103 mg	Sodium

SERVES 6 | MEAT · DON'T FREEZE

Creamy Chicken Rice Soup

6 cups | 1.5 L chicken stock

½ small onion, peeled and chopped ¼ inch | 5 mm thick

1 stalk celery, chopped into ¼-inch | 5-mm cubes

2 medium carrots, peeled and chopped into
¼-inch | 5-mm cubes

½ cup | 125 mL white rice

½ lb. | 250 g boneless, skinless chicken breast, cut into
½ -inch | 1-cm cubes

½ cup | 125 mL frozen peas

1 tsp. | 5 mL salt

¼ tsp. | 1 mL black pepper

¼ cup | 50 mL all-purpose flour

1 cup + 2 Tbsp. | 275 mL coffee creamer, non-dairy

This soup benefits from using real chicken stock. You can add any vegetables you like—mushrooms and frozen corn are two great additions. Cooking the chicken breast for only a few minutes at the end keeps it from getting dry, but make sure it is cooked through before eating!

METHOD

Over high heat bring chicken stock to a boil. Add onion, celery, carrots and rice. Cover and lower the heat so that the soup simmers gently and cook for 20 minutes, or until the rice is slightly underdone.

Add chicken breast, frozen peas, salt and pepper and simmer another 2–3 minutes.

In a separate bowl, whisk together flour and coffee creamer, making sure to remove all lumps. Add this mixture to the soup, stirring as you pour to ensure that it is well incorporated. Allow the soup to cook another 2–3 minutes until it has thickened and the chicken is cooked.

PER SERVING

312	Calories
11 g	Fat (31.9% calories from fat)
17 g	Protein
36 g	Carbohydrate
2 g	Dietary Fiber
23 mg	Cholesterol
1213 mg	Sodium

SERVES 6 | MEAT · FREEZES

❧ Italian Meatball Soup

MEATBALLS

1 lb. | 500 g ground chicken, dark meat

1 clove garlic (½ tsp. | 2 mL), crushed

½ tsp. | 2 mL dried oregano

½ tsp. | 2 mL dried basil

1 tsp. | 5 mL salt

⅛ tsp. | .5 mL black pepper

¼ cup | 50 mL dry bread crumbs

1 egg

SOUP

4 cups | 1 L chicken stock

2 cups | 500 mL water

1 small carrot, peeled and cut in half lengthwise and then into ¼ -inch | 5-mm half-circles

½ cup | 125 mL orzo

1 cup | 250 mL firmly packed spinach leaves (2 oz. | 50 g), cut into ¼-inch | 5-mm strips

1 tsp. | 5 mL salt

¼ tsp. | 1 mL black pepper

SERVES 6 | MEAT · FREEZES

I like to use ground chicken for these meatballs to keep the soup lighter. My homemade chicken stock (see page 110) is rich, so I add some water to this recipe. Taste your chicken soup before adding the water—if it is already lightly flavored, use 6 cups (1.5 L) of stock and forgo the water.

METHOD

Preheat the oven to 400°F (200°C). In a mixing bowl, combine all of the meatball ingredients and make sure everything is well incorporated. Use a tablespoon to measure the meatballs, rolling them into balls. If you find the mixture is sticking to your hands, dip them in cold water before shaping the meatballs. I like the meatballs to be pretty small, but you can make them any size you like. Place the meatballs on a baking sheet lined with parchment paper and bake for 10–13 minutes, until they are cooked through. If you make the meatballs a different size, check them while they are baking and take them out when they are just done, with no pink in the center when you cut one in half. Set the meatballs aside.

Bring the chicken stock and water (if using) to a boil, covered, over high heat. Turn the heat down to medium-low, add the carrot and orzo and simmer for 8 minutes.

Add the cooked meatballs and spinach and simmer just long enough to warm the meatballs and wilt the spinach.

Season with salt and pepper and serve!

PER SERVING

264	Calories
9 g	Fat (31.7% calories from fat)
29 g	Protein
14 g	Carbohydrate
1 g	Dietary Fiber
102 mg	Cholesterol
1351 mg	Sodium

Mexican Corn and Chicken Chowder

1 small yellow onion, peeled and finely chopped

1 stalk celery, sliced ¼ inch | 5 mm thick

2 Tbsp. | 25 mL olive oil

1 Tbsp. | 15 mL ground cumin

1 Tbsp. | 15 mL ground coriander

1 Tbsp. | 15 mL chili powder

1 tsp. | 5 mL salt

¼ tsp. | 1 mL black pepper

1 whole jalapeno, cored, seeded and finely chopped

1 can (28 oz. | 796 mL) diced tomatoes

2 Tbsp. | 25 mL tomato paste

4 cups | 1 L water

½ lb. | 250 g boneless, skinless chicken breast, cut into
½-inch | 1-cm cubes

1½ cups | 375 mL frozen corn kernels

1 Tbsp. | 15 mL cilantro, finely chopped

The corn brings a fresh sweetness to this chowder, cutting through the spices and heat. If you have fresh corn available, by all means use it!

METHOD

Over medium heat, sauté onion and celery in olive oil for 5–7 minutes, until the vegetables are wilted, but not browned.

Add the spices and jalapeno and sauté another minute, stirring constantly.

Add tomatoes, tomato paste and water. Cover and turn up the heat to bring the soup to a boil. Once it reaches a boil, reduce heat and simmer the soup for 20 minutes on medium-low.

Add the cubed chicken and frozen corn and simmer another 5 minutes, or until the chicken is cooked through.

Add cilantro and serve.

PER SERVING

168	Calories
7 g	Fat (32.7% calories from fat)
12 g	Protein
19 g	Carbohydrate
4 g	Dietary Fiber
23 mg	Cholesterol
646 mg	Sodium

SERVES 6 | MEAT · FREEZES

Roasted Rosemary Chicken Soup

1 large carrot, peeled and cut into ½-inch | 1-cm cubes

3 stalks celery, cut into ½-inch | 1-cm cubes

1 small red onion, peeled and cut into ½-inch | 1-cm cubes

6 oz. | 175 g mushrooms, quartered

2 Tbsp. | 25 mL olive oil

5 large garlic cloves, thinly sliced

1½ tsp. | 7 mL fresh rosemary, finely chopped

1½ tsp. | 7 mL salt

½ tsp. | 2 mL black pepper

about 3 chicken legs (2 lbs. | 1 kg), skin on

¾ lb. | 375 g chicken necks

8 cups | 2 L water

Roasting the vegetables and chicken first adds a ton of flavor to this soup. The slices of garlic sweeten as they roast and melt into the soup.

METHOD

Preheat the oven to 425°F (220°C). In a large roasting pan, place the carrot, celery, onion, mushrooms, olive oil, garlic, 1 tsp. (5 mL) rosemary, 1 tsp. (5 mL) salt and ¼ tsp. (1 mL) pepper. Toss everything together so that all of the vegetables are lightly coated in oil and seasonings. Place the cleaned chicken legs and necks on top of the vegetables, in a single layer, skin-side up. Sprinkle the chicken with ½ tsp. (2 mL) salt, ½ tsp. (2 mL) rosemary and ¼ tsp. (1 mL) pepper. Roast for 40 minutes, until the skin is crispy and golden brown.

Pull the pan out of the oven and immediately place the chicken in a dish to cool in the refrigerator. Strain the vegetables well, trying to get as much of the juices out of them as possible. Place the vegetables in a dish and refrigerate to cool. Pour the liquid into a bowl and refrigerate until cold. The fat will rise to the top.

When the liquid has completely cooled, and there is a hard layer of chicken fat on top, carefully scoop the fat off and discard. Place the leftover juices in a soup pot.

Pull the skin off the chicken legs and discard. Next pull the meat off and shred into large chunks. Reserve for later. Add the chicken bones and water to the juices in the pot and bring to a boil, covered, over high heat. Reduce heat and simmer for 1 hour.

Remove the bones from the soup and discard. Add the reserved chicken meat and vegetables to the soup and simmer just long enough to heat through. Serve!

PER SERVING

255	Calories
17 g	Fat (61.4% calories from fat)
16 g	Protein
8 g	Carbohydrate
2 g	Dietary Fiber
70 mg	Cholesterol
633 mg	Sodium

SERVES 6 | MEAT · FREEZES · PASSOVER

Thai Chicken and Coconut Soup

3 1-inch | 2.5-cm pieces lemon grass

1 cup | 250 mL water

4 cups | 1 L chicken stock

1–2 cloves garlic (1 tsp. | 5 mL), crushed

1 tsp. | 5 mL fresh ginger, finely minced

1 whole red chili pepper, cored, seeded and finely minced

1 can (14 oz. | 398 mL) coconut milk

¼ lb. | 125 g button mushrooms, sliced
¼ inch | 5 mm thick

1 small carrot, peeled and cut into matchsticks

1 tsp. | 5 mL sambal oelek (chili sauce)

¼ small red onion, peeled and cut into thin strips

¼ lb. | 125 g rice noodles (pad Thai or fettuccini)

10 oz. | 300 g boneless, skinless chicken breast, cut into
¼-inch | 5-mm strips

1 cup | 250 mL bean sprouts

1 Tbsp. | 15 mL cilantro, finely chopped

1 Tbsp. | 15 mL soy sauce

1–2 green onions (scallions), thinly sliced

1 Tbsp. | 15 mL fresh lime juice

1 tsp. | 5 mL salt

SERVES 6 | MEAT · DON'T FREEZE

This soup bursts with different flavors. The coconut milk is rich and creamy, the lemon grass and lime add a hint of sour and the chili pepper, ginger and sambal oelek bring the heat.

METHOD

Smash the lemon grass with a kitchen mallet or carefully under a knife to break up some of the fibers and release the flavor. Place water, chicken stock, garlic, ginger, lemon grass and chili pepper into a soup pot, cover and bring to a boil over high heat.

Add the coconut milk, mushrooms, carrot, sambal oelek and red onion, allow to come back up to a simmer and simmer gently for 3–5 minutes.

If you are using the pad Thai rice noodles, or the fettuccini rice noodles, add them now and cook another 5–7 minutes. If you are using a different noodle shape, follow the directions on the package and add them at the end, already cooked. If you don't add the noodles now, you still need to simmer the soup another 5–7 minutes.

Add the chicken strips and cook 2–3 minutes, or until the chicken is almost cooked through.

Add the bean sprouts and continue simmering until the chicken is fully cooked.

Just before serving, remove the lemon grass and add the cilantro, soy sauce, green onion and lime juice.

Check for salt and serve.

PER SERVING

322	Calories
18 g	Fat (49.2% calories from fat)
17 g	Protein
25 g	Carbohydrate
3 g	Dietary Fiber
29 mg	Cholesterol
1080 mg	Sodium

Thai Ginger Chicken Soup

½ small yellow onion, peeled and thinly sliced

2 Tbsp. | 25 mL olive oil

1 small carrot, peeled and cut into matchsticks

3 oz. | 75 g mushrooms, cut in ¼-inch | 5-mm slices

2 Tbsp. | 25 mL fresh ginger, finely minced

4–6 cloves garlic (1 Tbsp. | 15 mL), crushed

6 cups | 1.5 L chicken stock

½ lb. | 250 g boneless, skinless chicken breast, cut into thin strips

2 Tbsp. | 25 mL soy sauce

3 green onions (scallions), sliced on the diagonal in ½-inch | 1-cm pieces

¼ cup | 50 mL canned bamboo shoots

1 tsp. | 5 mL dark sesame oil

Add some cooked rice or rice noodles and this is a perfect meal.

METHOD

Sauté onion in olive oil over medium-low heat for 5 minutes.

Add carrot and mushrooms and sauté another 3–4 minutes, until the mushrooms start releasing their juices.

Add ginger and garlic and sauté another 30 seconds, stirring constantly.

Add stock, cover and bring to a boil over high heat. Reduce heat to medium-low. Add the chicken breast strips and simmer for 2–3 minutes.

Add soy sauce, green onions and bamboo shoots and simmer 3–4 minutes to heat through and finish cooking the chicken.

Add sesame oil just before serving.

PER SERVING

151	Calories
8 g	Fat (47.0% calories from fat)
14 g	Protein
5 g	Carbohydrate
1 g	Dietary Fiber
23 mg	Cholesterol
1132 mg	Sodium

SERVES 6 | MEAT · FREEZES

Bread and Tomato Soup

1 small yellow onion, peeled and finely chopped

3 Tbsp. | 45 mL olive oil

6–9 cloves garlic (1½ Tbsp. | 20 mL), crushed

4–5 medium Roma (Italian plum) tomatoes, peeled and chopped into small cubes

5 cups | 1.25 L chicken stock

½ tsp. | 2 mL salt

⅛ tsp. | .5 mL black pepper

4 slices French bread, dried

½ cup | 125 mL fresh basil (firmly packed), sliced into thin strips

Day-old bread works best for this. Leave the slices on a baking sheet uncovered for at least an hour before you are ready to serve. The dry bread absorbs the stock and melts into the soup. I prefer this soup made with real chicken stock. My mother likes using a parve stock and adding some Parmesan cheese at the end. Try it both ways and see which you prefer.

METHOD

In a soup pot, over low heat, sauté the onion in olive oil until it softens, but does not brown, 8–10 minutes.

Add the crushed garlic and continue cooking for another 30 seconds or so. The heat should be low enough that the garlic doesn't brown.

Add the tomatoes and sauté for 2–3 minutes.

Add the chicken stock, salt and pepper and bring to a boil. Simmer 15 minutes.

In the bottom of four soup bowls, place one slice of the dry bread and a quarter of the basil. Pour the soup over the bread and serve.

PER SERVING

217	Calories
11 g	Fat (50.2% calories from fat)
4 g	Protein
21 g	Carbohydrate
2 g	Dietary Fiber
0 mg	Cholesterol
3111 mg	Sodium

SERVES 4 | MEAT · DON'T FREEZE

Garlic Soup

8–12 cloves garlic (2 Tbsp. | 25 mL), crushed

2 Tbsp. | 25 mL olive oil

6 cups | 1.5 L chicken stock

2 medium Roma (Italian plum) tomatoes, cored, seeded and diced into ¼-inch | 5-mm cubes

3 eggs, beaten

½ tsp. | 2 mL salt

¼ tsp. | 1 mL black pepper

Perfect for garlic lovers, this soup is great with fresh, crusty bread to dip in and absorb all the wonderful garlic flavor. Although I think this soup tastes best with real chicken stock, you could substitute a different stock if you prefer.

METHOD

Over very low heat, sauté the garlic in olive oil for 1–2 minutes. The point here is not to brown the garlic, but for the olive oil to absorb all of the garlic flavor. As soon as you see the garlic start to pick up any color, go on to the next step.

Add the chicken stock, cover and turn the heat up to bring the soup to a boil. Turn the heat down so that the soup simmers gently. Allow to simmer for 2–3 minutes on low.

Add the tomatoes and simmer another minute or two.

In a slow, thin stream, pour the beaten eggs into the soup —leave it about 10 seconds before stirring. Season with salt and pepper and serve!

PER SERVING

121	Calories
8 g	Fat (62.0% calories from fat)
8 g	Protein
3 g	Carbohydrate
trace	Dietary Fiber
94 mg	Cholesterol
971 mg	Sodium

SERVES 6 | MEAT · DON'T FREEZE · PASSOVER

Greek Lemon Rice Soup (Avgolemono)

6 cups | 1.5 L chicken stock

¾ cup | 175 mL white rice

2 Tbsp. | 25 mL all-purpose flour

2 lemons, juiced

3 eggs

¼ tsp. | 1 mL salt

1 pinch black pepper

No substitutes—you need to use real chicken stock for this one! Whisking the egg in toward the end thickens the soup and gives it a nice, creamy consistency.

METHOD

Bring the chicken stock to a simmer and add the rice. Simmer, covered, until the rice is tender, approximately 20 minutes.

In a separate bowl, whisk together the flour, lemon juice, eggs, salt and pepper. As you continue to whisk the mixture, slowly add some of the hot soup. This will prevent the eggs from scrambling when you add the mixture into the pot. Add about 1 cup (250 mL) of hot liquid to the egg mixture.

While whisking the soup, slowly pour in the egg mixture. Make sure the mixture gets well incorporated. Let the soup return to a simmer for approximately 5 minutes, allowing the eggs and flour to cook and thicken the soup.

PER SERVING

253	Calories
6 g	Fat (20.3% calories from fat)
15 g	Protein
36 g	Carbohydrate
1 g	Dietary Fiber
140 mg	Cholesterol
1322 mg	Sodium

SERVES 4 | MEAT · DON'T FREEZE

Tortilla Soup

2 7-inch flour tortillas

vegetable spray

1 small red onion, peeled and finely chopped

1 large jalapeno pepper, seeded, cored and finely diced

2 Tbsp. | 25 mL olive oil

1–2 cloves garlic (1 tsp. | 5 mL), crushed

2 tsp. | 10 mL ground cumin

1 tsp. | 5 mL salt

¼ tsp. | 1 mL black pepper

5 cups | 1.25 L stock

1 cup | 250 mL canned diced tomatoes

½ lb. | 250 g boneless, skinless chicken breasts, cut into ½-inch | 1-cm cubes

1 can (16 oz. or 19 oz. | 540 mL) black beans, rinsed and drained

¾ cup | 175 mL frozen corn kernels

1 Tbsp. | 15 mL fresh lime juice

1 tsp. | 5 mL hot sauce

2 Tbsp. | 25 mL cilantro (firmly packed), chopped

The lime juice and cilantro give this soup an amazing fresh flavor. For a vegetarian alternative, leave out the chicken breast and add some shredded cheddar cheese and sour cream.

METHOD

Preheat the oven to 350°F (180°C). Spray both sides of the tortillas lightly with vegetable spray, then cut into ¼-inch by 1½-inch (5-mm by 4-cm) strips. Spread the strips in a single layer on a parchment-lined baking sheet and bake for 4–6 minutes, until crisp and lightly browned.

Over medium-low heat, sauté the onion and jalapeno in olive oil for 5–8 minutes, until soft.

Add the garlic, cumin, salt and pepper and cook another 30 seconds, stirring constantly.

Add stock and tomatoes and bring to a boil, covered, over high heat. Reduce heat and simmer for 15 minutes on medium-low.

Add the chicken and beans, cook 2 minutes and add the corn. Cook another 3–5 minutes, until the corn is warmed through and the chicken is fully cooked.

Add lime juice and hot sauce just before serving. Top each bowl with cilantro and tortilla strips.

PER SERVING

277	Calories
8 g	Fat (27.1% calories from fat)
17 g	Protein
34 g	Carbohydrate
7 g	Dietary Fiber
23 mg	Cholesterol
793 mg	Sodium

SERVES 6 | MEAT · FREEZE WITHOUT TORTILLAS

Shredded Duck Soup

3-lb. | 1.5-kg duck (whole)

1 tsp. | 5 mL salt

¼ tsp. | 1 mL black pepper

8 cups | 2 L water

½ oz. | 15 g dried shiitake mushrooms

1 cup | 250 mL boiling water

¼ cup | 50 mL canned bamboo shoots

1 Tbsp. | 15 mL hoisin sauce

2 Tbsp. | 25 mL soy sauce

3 Tbsp. | 45 mL cornstarch

1 cup | 250 mL cold water

1 cup | 250 mL bean sprouts

1 tsp. | 5 mL salt

¼ tsp. | 1 mL black pepper

1–2 green onions (scallions), thinly sliced

This is not a soup to make on the spur of the moment, but it is rich and amazingly flavorful. It is important to remove as much of the fat as possible or your final soup will be greasy.

METHOD

Preheat oven to 400°F (200°C). Cut slits about ⅛ inch (3 mm) deep into the skin over the breasts of a well washed and dried duck then sprinkle with 1 tsp. (5 mL) of salt and ¼ tsp. (1 mL) of black pepper. This will allow the fat to cook out of the duck as it's roasting. Place a rack in a roasting pan and put the duck onto the rack, breast up. Cover the pan with aluminum foil and roast for 45 minutes. Remove the foil and continue to roast another 25–30 minutes, until the skin is golden brown, the juices run clear when you cut into the leg joint and

almost all of the fat has cooked out of the duck. Set the duck aside until it is cool enough for you to handle.

Remove and discard all the duck skin and fat. Take all the meat that you can off the duck carcass. You should get approximately 1 pound (500 g). Shred the meat into strips and reserve.

Place the duck bones and 8 cups (2 L) of cold water into a soup pot over high heat, cover and bring to a boil. Reduce the heat and simmer for 1 hour, skimming off any scum.

While the soup is simmering, rinse the shiitake mushrooms well and place in a bowl with 1 cup (250 mL) of boiling water. Cover with plastic wrap and set aside. When the water has cooled enough to handle, pull out the mushrooms and slice into strips. Reserve both the liquid and the mushrooms.

After the duck bones have simmered for an hour, pull the bones out and discard. Add the shiitake water, pouring slowly to ensure that any residue will remain in the bottom of the bowl. Add the mushrooms, the duck meat, bamboo shoots and hoisin sauce and soy sauce and simmer for 5 minutes.

In a separate bowl, whisk together the cornstarch and remaining 1 cup (250 mL) of cold water. Whisk this mixture into the soup and simmer another minute.

Add the bean sprouts, 1 tsp. (5 mL) salt and ¼ tsp. (1 mL) black pepper and simmer another minute. Top each bowl of soup with green onion.

PER SERVING	
124	Calories
5 g	Fat (34.7% calories from fat)
15 g	Protein
5 g	Carbohydrate
1 g	Dietary Fiber
60 mg	Cholesterol
1167 mg	Sodium

SERVES 6 | MEAT • DON'T FREEZE

Smoked Duck Soup with Wild Rice

3-lb. | 1.5-kg smoked duck

10 cups | 2.5 L cold water

1 small yellow onion, peeled and finely chopped

1 stalk celery, finely chopped

2 cups | 500 mL cooked wild rice

1½ tsp. | 7 mL salt

¼ tsp. | 1 mL black pepper

½ cup | 125 mL dried cranberries

This is a soup right out of the Prairies. If you can purchase smoked duck, use that. If not, place a foil pan with wet wood chips on one side of your barbeque with the heat on underneath, and place the duck on a rack inside a pan on the other side of the barbeque with that side turned off. A 3-pound (1.5 kg) duck will take about 1½ hours, depending on the temperature of your barbeque. Check it occasionally—the duck will be cooked if the liquid runs clear when you cut into the leg joint.

METHOD

Remove all skin and fat from the duck. Discard. Remove the duck meat and reserve. Place the duck carcass in a soup pot with the water. Cover and place over high heat and bring to a boil. Reduce the heat and allow to simmer for 1 hour with the lid on and 15 minutes with the lid removed, skimming off any residue.

Remove the duck bones and discard. Add the onion and celery and simmer, covered, for 10 minutes.

Dice the reserved duck meat into ½-inch (1-cm) cubes. Add to the soup along with the rice, salt, pepper and cranberries and simmer for 10–15 minutes.

PER SERVING

141	Calories
4 g	Fat (23.4% calories from fat)
13 g	Protein
14 g	Carbohydrate
2 g	Dietary Fiber
45 mg	Cholesterol
462 mg	Sodium

SERVES 8 | MEAT · FREEZES

Chicken Soup with Fresh Herbs #1 | *page 111*

Asian Chicken Noodle Soup Bowl | *page 113*

Tortilla Soup | *page 126*

Greek Meatball Soup | *page 140*

Ten Bean Soup (with Smoked Turkey)

2 Tbsp. | 25 mL lima beans

2 Tbsp. | 25 mL kidney beans

2 Tbsp. | 25 mL black beans

2 Tbsp. | 25 mL pinto beans

2 Tbsp. | 25 mL navy beans

2 Tbsp. | 25 mL black-eyed peas

2 Tbsp. | 25 mL yellow split peas

2 Tbsp. | 25 mL green split peas

¼ cup | 50 mL green lentils

¼ cup | 50 mL red lentils

water for soaking beans

1 bay leaf

8 cups | 2 L stock

1 lb. | 500 g smoked turkey wings

2 stalks celery, chopped

1 small yellow onion, peeled and finely chopped

¼ lb. | 125 g button mushrooms, sliced ¼ inch | 5 mm thick

1 medium carrot, peeled and finely chopped

¼ tsp. | 1 mL black pepper

1½ tsp. | 7 mL salt

There are certain soups I like more than others. Same goes for my mother, father, staff at work and friends. This is one soup we all tasted and went "Ah, this is good." The smoked turkey and beans are perfect partners.

METHOD

Pick through the beans, making sure there are no stones or any other debris. Thoroughly rinse the beans (use a colander) and place them in a deep bowl or pot. Cover with a minimum of 8 cups (2 L) of water, cover loosely with plastic wrap or wax paper and let sit overnight.

After a minimum of 12 hours, drain and rinse the beans and put them in a pot along with the bay leaf, stock and smoked turkey wings. Cover the pot and bring to a boil over high heat, covered. Reduce heat and simmer for 30 minutes over medium-low heat.

Add all of the vegetables, pepper and salt and simmer another 30 minutes, until the vegetables and beans are tender.

Remove bay leaf. Take the turkey wings out of the soup and carefully remove the skin. Pull the turkey meat from the bones, and either shred it by hand or cut into small cubes. Discard the skin and bones. Return the meat to the soup, heat through and serve.

PER SERVING

202	Calories
5 g	Fat (20.9% calories from fat)
16 g	Protein
24 g	Carbohydrate
9 g	Dietary Fiber
19 mg	Cholesterol
1537 mg	Sodium

SERVES 10 | MEAT • FREEZES

Turkey and Wild Rice Soup

2 lbs. | 1 kg turkey wings, well washed

10 cups | 2.5 L cold water

1 small yellow onion, peeled and finely chopped

1 stalk celery, sliced ⅛ inch | 3 mm thick

1 small carrot, peeled and cut into ¼-inch | 5-mm cubes

2 cups | 500 mL cooked wild rice

1½ cups | 375 mL non-dairy coffee creamer

6 Tbsp. | 90 mL all-purpose flour

2½ tsp. | 12 mL salt

½ tsp. | 2 mL black pepper

¼ cup | 50 mL slivered almonds, toasted

Rich, creamy and full of different textures. Make this soup for a special treat.

METHOD

Place the turkey wings and cold water in a covered soup pot over high heat and bring to a boil. Reduce the heat and simmer on medium-low for 1 hour, skimming off any scum or foam that rises to the top.

Remove the turkey, setting aside to cool, and add onion, celery and carrot to the soup. Simmer an additional 15 minutes.

When you can handle the turkey, remove and discard the skin and bones. Cut the turkey meat into ½-inch (1-cm) cubes. Add to the soup along with the wild rice and simmer another 5 minutes.

In a separate bowl, whisk together the coffee creamer and flour. Whisk this mixture into the soup, add the salt and pepper and simmer 4–5 minutes.

Garnish each bowl of soup with some of the toasted slivered almonds.

PER SERVING

282	Calories
14 g	Fat (45.1% calories from fat)
16 g	Protein
23 g	Carbohydrate
2 g	Dietary Fiber
43 mg	Cholesterol
610 mg	Sodium

SERVES 10 | MEAT • FREEZES

Beef Stock

4 lbs. | 2 kg beef bones, fat removed

1 tsp. | 5 mL salt

½ tsp. | 2mL black pepper

16 cups | 4 L cold water

2 medium carrots, peeled and halved

4 stalks celery, halved

2 medium yellow onions, peeled and halved

½ tsp. | 2 mL black peppercorns

1 tsp. | 5 mL salt

Roasting the bones then simmering and reducing for four and a half hours produces a very rich stock. I generally use a stock like this one as a base for other soups.

METHOD

Preheat oven to 425°F (220°C). Place bones on cookie sheet lined with parchment paper. Sprinkle 1 tsp. (5 mL) of salt and ½ tsp. (2 mL) of black pepper over the bones. Roast for 45 minutes, turning once after 25 minutes.

Place bones and cold water in a large pot and bring to a boil over high heat. Reduce heat and simmer for half an hour, skimming off any residue or scum.

Add all of the vegetables, peppercorns and 1 tsp. (5 mL) salt. Simmer another 3 hours, uncovered. If the soup boils too briskly, you may need to add extra water. The soup should reduce, but you don't want it all to disappear.

Strain the soup through a fine mesh colander or cheesecloth and refrigerate. Once the soup is cold, any excess fat will have hardened and can be carefully skimmed off.

Reheat for serving or use in other recipes.

PER SERVING

38	Calories
trace	Fat (4.0% calories from fat)
1 g	Protein
9 g	Carbohydrate
2 g	Dietary Fiber
0 mg	Cholesterol
582 mg	Sodium

SERVES 8 | MEAT · FREEZES · PASSOVER

❧ Asian Beef Stock

6 cups | 1.5 L beef stock

½ tsp. | 2 mL fresh ginger, finely minced

1 clove garlic (½ tsp. | 2 mL), crushed

1 Tbsp. | 15 mL soy sauce, dark

3 green onions (scallions), finely sliced

Serve this with cooked white rice or homemade won-tons. Depending on the stock you use, you may find the soup too rich. Try adding a bit of water if that's the case, or even use homemade chicken stock for a lighter version.

METHOD

Bring stock, ginger, garlic and soy sauce to a boil and simmer 2–3 minutes.

Add green onion and serve.

PER SERVING

62	Calories
trace	Fat (0.1% calories from fat)
11 g	Protein
4 g	Carbohydrate
trace	Dietary Fiber
0 mg	Cholesterol
1451 mg	Sodium

SERVES 6 | MEAT • FREEZES

Asian Meatball Soup

Meatballs

1 lb. | 500 g lean ground beef

1–2 green onions (scallions), minced

1 tsp. | 5 mL sesame oil

2 tsp. | 10 mL soy sauce

1–2 cloves garlic (1 tsp. | 5 mL), crushed

1 tsp. | 5 mL fresh ginger, finely grated

1 egg white

¼ tsp. | 1 mL salt

⅛ tsp. | .5 mL black pepper

½ tsp. | 2 mL granulated sugar

Soup

6 cups | 1.5 L chicken stock

1 cup | 250 mL water

½ cup | 125 mL white rice

2 Tbsp. | 25 mL soy sauce

1 small carrot, julienned

1 stalk celery, julienned

1–2 green onions (scallions), thinly sliced

1 tsp. | 5 mL sesame oil

Serve smaller portions for a starter, or add some broccoli, cauliflower and pea pods for a complete dinner.

METHOD

Preheat the oven to 350°F (180°C). For the meatballs, mix together all of the ingredients. Make sure everything is well blended, then start forming the balls. I like them to be rather small and use approximately 1 tsp. (5 mL) for each ball. Roll the meat mixture between your hands to form them, dipping your hands in cold water if you find that the meat is sticking. Place the meatballs on a baking sheet lined with parchment paper or aluminum foil, and bake for 10 minutes. The meatballs will continue to cook in the soup, but they should be almost done at this point. Drain the hot meatballs on paper towels so the excess fat is removed. Set aside.

Bring the chicken stock and water to a boil over high heat, covered. Add the rice, soy sauce and meatballs. Turn the heat down so the soup simmers gently and cook for 10 minutes.

Add the carrot and celery and simmer an additional 10 minutes, or until the rice is cooked.

Garnish with the green onion and sesame oil and serve.

PER SERVING

323	Calories
19 g	Fat (53.4% calories from fat)
21 g	Protein
16 g	Carbohydrate
1 g	Dietary Fiber
57 mg	Cholesterol
1384 mg	Sodium

SERVES 6 | MEAT · FREEZES

Beef and Barley Soup

¾ lb. | 375 g stewing beef, cut into ½-inch | 1-cm cubes

10 cups | 2.5 L water

1 small yellow onion, finely chopped

2 stalks celery, finely chopped

1 large carrot, peeled and finely chopped

6 oz. | 175 g button mushrooms, thinly sliced

⅜ cup | 80 mL pearl barley, rinsed

1½ tsp. | 7 mL salt

¼ tsp. | 1 mL black pepper

For me, this is the perfect one-dish meal. Protein, vegetable and starch! Tasty and filling.

METHOD

Place the beef and water in a soup pot and bring to a boil on high, skimming off any foam or residue. Reduce heat to medium and simmer for 10 minutes, skimming all along, until the liquid is clear and there is nothing more to skim.

Add the vegetables, barley, salt and pepper, cover and simmer gently for 45 minutes, until the barley is cooked and tender.

PER SERVING

60	Calories
trace	Fat (3.7% calories from fat)
2 g	Protein
13 g	Carbohydrate
3 g	Dietary Fiber
0 mg	Cholesterol
429 mg	Sodium

SERVES 8 | DAIRY · FREEZES

Beef and Macaroni Soup

1 lb. | 500 g lean ground beef

1 medium yellow onion, peeled and finely chopped

2 Tbsp. | 25 mL olive oil

½ small red pepper, cored, seeded and diced

1 small piece cabbage, shredded

4–6 cloves garlic (1 Tbsp. | 15 mL), crushed

1½ tsp. | 7 mL dried oregano

1½ tsp. | 7 mL dried basil

2 tsp. | 10 mL salt

1 tsp. | 5 mL black pepper

1 Tbsp. | 15 mL granulated sugar

1 can (16 oz. or 19 oz. | 540 mL) kidney beans, rinsed and drained

1 can (28 oz. | 796 mL) crushed tomatoes

8 cups | 2 L water

¾ cup | 175 mL macaroni

Another fantastic one-bowl meal, although I do enjoy it with a crisp salad.

METHOD

Over medium-high heat, sauté ground beef in a dry, non-stick frying pan until it is cooked through and there is no pink left. Set aside in a colander to drain.

In a soup pot, sweat the onion in the olive oil over medium heat for 2–3 minutes.

Add pepper and cabbage and sauté another 5 minutes.

Add seasonings and continue cooking another 1–2 minutes.

Add the cooked, drained beef, beans, tomatoes and water and bring to a boil over high heat. Reduce heat to medium and allow to simmer for 10 minutes.

Add the pasta, continue simmering until it is tender and serve! (Timing will depend on the pasta shape—follow package directions for cooking time.)

PER SERVING

214	Calories
11 g	Fat (43.9% calories from fat)
11 g	Protein
19 g	Carbohydrate
5 g	Dietary Fiber
28 mg	Cholesterol
640 mg	Sodium

SERVES 12 | MEAT · FREEZES

Beef and Vegetable Stew Soup

1 Tbsp. | 15 mL all-purpose flour

2 tsp. | 10 mL salt

¾ tsp. | 4 mL black pepper

¾ lb. | 375 g stewing beef, cut in ½-inch | 1-cm cubes

3 Tbsp. | 45 mL olive oil

7 cups | 1.75 L cold water

1 can (28 oz. | 796 mL) diced tomatoes

1–2 cloves garlic (1 tsp. | 5 mL), crushed

¾ tsp. | 4 mL dried thyme

1 medium carrot, peeled and cut in ½-inch | 1-cm cubes

1 small yellow onion, peeled and coarsely chopped

1 stalk celery, cut into ½-inch | 1-cm cubes

¼ lb. | 125 g button mushrooms, sliced ¼ inch | 5 mm thick

1 large red potato, peeled and cut in ½-inch | 1-cm cubes

3 Tbsp. | 45 mL all-purpose flour

1 cup | 250 mL cold water

Is it a soup or a stew? Well, maybe it's both. Serve with rustic bread for a hearty meal.

METHOD

In a bowl, mix the flour, 1 tsp. (5 mL) salt and ½ tsp. (2 mL) black pepper together. Toss the beef in this mixture so that it is all lightly dusted with the flour and spices.

Over medium-high heat, sauté the meat in olive oil until it is lightly browned. Add 7 cups (1.75 L) cold water and bring to a boil. Simmer for approximately 10 minutes, skimming off any foam and scum.

Add the canned tomatoes, garlic and thyme. Cover and allow to simmer over medium-low heat for 30 minutes.

Add all the vegetables and the remaining salt and black pepper. Simmer another 40 minutes.

In a separate bowl, whisk together 3 Tbsp. (45 mL) of flour and 1 cup (250 mL) of cold water. Whisk this mixture into the soup and allow the soup to simmer and thicken, another 3–5 minutes.

PER SERVING

245	Calories
11 g	Fat (41.2% calories from fat)
13 g	Protein
23 g	Carbohydrate
4 g	Dietary Fiber
26 mg	Cholesterol
781 mg	Sodium

SERVES 6 | MEAT · FREEZES

Beef Eggdrop Soup

5 cups | 1.25 L beef stock

2 oz. | 50 g mushrooms, thinly sliced

¼ small yellow onion, thinly sliced

½ small carrot, peeled and cut into matchstick pieces

2 Tbsp. | 25 mL soy sauce

¼ cup | 50 mL canned bamboo shoots, drained

¼ lb. | 125 g beef rib eye, sliced ⅛ inch | 3 mm thick

2 Tbsp. | 25 mL cornstarch

½ cup | 125 mL cold water

2 eggs

1 Tbsp. | 15 mL sesame oil

½ tsp. | 2 mL salt

¼ tsp. | 1 mL black pepper

1–2 green onions (scallions), thinly sliced

This is a great starter. It's on the rich side though, so you may want to try it before using it for a main course! The beef should be sliced very thin. If you have difficulty slicing the meat, place it in the freezer for about half an hour then slice with a sharp knife.

METHOD

Over high heat, bring the beef stock to a boil. Add the mushrooms, yellow onion and carrot. Turn the heat down and simmer about 8 minutes, uncovered.

Add the soy sauce, bamboo shoots and rib eye and simmer for another minute.

In a separate bowl, whisk together the cornstarch and cold water. Add this mixture to the soup, whisk in and continue to simmer. After 2–3 minutes the soup should thicken.

In another bowl, whisk together the eggs and the sesame oil. With the soup gently simmering, pour this mixture in a slow stream into the soup. Give the soup a stir to break up the egg strands.

Season with salt and pepper. Garnish with green onion and serve.

PER SERVING

152	Calories
8 g	Fat (44.3% calories from fat)
15 g	Protein
5 g	Carbohydrate
1 g	Dietary Fiber
75 mg	Cholesterol
1619 mg	Sodium

SERVES 6 | MEAT · DON'T FREEZE

Cabbage Roll Soup

1 lb. | 500 g lean ground beef

1 small yellow onion, peeled and finely chopped

3 tsp. | 15 mL salt

½ tsp. | 2 mL black pepper

2 Tbsp. | 25 mL olive oil

½ small green cabbage (¾ lb. | 375 g), finely shredded

5 Tbsp. | 75 mL tomato paste

1 can (28 oz. | 796 mL) diced tomatoes

10 cups | 2.5 L water

½ cup | 125 mL white rice

This tastes just like my grandmother's cabbage rolls, but takes much less time to prepare. You can substitute ground chicken for a lighter version.

METHOD

Sauté the beef in a dry, non-stick frying pan over medium-high heat until it is cooked through and there is no more pink. Drain the meat and set aside.

In a pot, sauté the onion, salt and pepper in olive oil over medium-low heat for 5–8 minutes, until the onion is soft.

Add the cabbage and sauté for 3–5 minutes, until it starts to wilt.

Add the beef, tomato paste, diced tomatoes and water. Cover the pot and bring to a boil over high heat. Reduce the heat and simmer gently for half an hour.

Add the rice and simmer for another 20 minutes, or until the rice is tender.

PER SERVING

223	Calories
13 g	Fat (50.2% calories from fat)
10 g	Protein
18 g	Carbohydrate
2 g	Dietary Fiber
34 mg	Cholesterol
757 mg	Sodium

SERVES 10 | MEAT · FREEZES

Chili Soup

1½ lbs. | 750 g extra-lean ground beef

1 small yellow onion, finely chopped

1 medium carrot, peeled and grated

1 stalk celery, finely chopped

1 medium red pepper, cored, seeded and finely chopped

¼ cup | 50 mL olive oil

1½ tsp. | 7 mL salt

4–6 cloves garlic (1 Tbsp. | 15 mL), crushed

¼ tsp. | 1 mL pepper

1½ Tbsp. | 20 mL ground cumin

1 tsp. | 5 mL ground coriander

1½ Tbsp. | 20 mL chili powder

1 can (28 oz. | 796 mL) diced tomatoes

1 can (12 oz. | 375 mL) corn kernels, rinsed and drained

1 can (16 oz. or 19 oz. | 540 mL) red kidney beans, rinsed and drained

1 can (16 oz. or 19 oz. | 540 mL) black beans, rinsed and drained

¼ tsp. | 1 mL hot sauce

6 cups | 1.5 L water

As a great alternative, substitute ground chicken for the beef—or leave out the meat altogether as a vegetarian option. Garnish with taco chips to serve.

METHOD

I usually sauté ground beef in a dry, non-stick frying pan over medium heat, but since this is extra-lean beef, add a little oil to start it off. Sauté the beef until all the pink is gone, then drain off the extra liquid and set aside.

Over medium heat, in a soup pot, sauté all the vegetables for 5 minutes in the olive oil. The vegetables will wilt, but don't let them brown.

Add all the seasonings and sauté an additional minute.

Add the beef, tomatoes, corn, beans, hot sauce and water, cover and bring to a boil. Simmer approximately 25 minutes and the soup is done!

PER SERVING

299	Calories
15 g	Fat (45.5% calories from fat)
17 g	Protein
24 g	Carbohydrate
8 g	Dietary Fiber
39 mg	Cholesterol
778 mg	Sodium

SERVES 12 | MEAT • FREEZES

Greek Meatball Soup

¾ cup | 175 mL white rice, reserved for meatballs and soup (will yield 2 cups | 500 mL of cooked rice)

MEATBALLS

1½ lbs. | 750 g lean ground beef

½ cup | 125 mL reserved rice

1 egg

2–4 cloves garlic (2 tsp. | 10 mL), crushed

1 tsp. | 5 mL dried oregano

1½ tsp. | 7 mL salt

½ tsp. | 2 mL black pepper

1 small yellow onion, chopped fine and sautéed in 1 tsp. | 5 mL olive oil

1 tsp. | 5 mL lemon juice

1 tsp. | 5 mL red wine vinegar

1 Tbsp. | 15 mL olive oil

SOUP

½ small yellow onion, diced small

2 Tbsp. | 25 mL olive oil

1 medium red pepper, cored and cubed ½ inch | 1 cm thick

6 oz. | 175 g mushrooms, sliced ¼ inch | 5 mm thick

8–12 cloves garlic (2 Tbsp. | 25 mL), crushed

1 can (28 oz. | 796 mL) crushed tomatoes

1 large zucchini, diced ¼ inch | 5 mm thick

6 cups | 1.5 L water

1 Tbsp. | 15 mL granulated sugar

1 tsp. | 5 mL salt

½ tsp. | 2 mL black pepper

1⅓ Tbsp. | 20 mL dried oregano

1½ cups | 375 mL reserved rice

¼ cup | 50 mL lemon juice

Use ground chicken or lamb instead of beef for a nice variation.

METHOD

Cook the white rice until tender, then chill. Half a cup (125 mL) of the cooked rice will go into the meatballs, the rest will be added to the soup at the end.

In a bowl, combine all of the meatball ingredients. Make sure the mixture is well mixed, then form the meatballs. I like to make them bite-sized so they don't need any cutting, but you can make them any size you like. If the meat sticks to your hands, dip your hands into cold water as you work. When the meatballs are formed, chill them in the freezer for about half an hour so they firm up before frying.

Over high heat, use enough oil in a frying pan to lightly coat it (about 1 Tbsp. | 15 mL). Add as many meatballs as it takes to have a single, uncluttered layer. Brown the meatballs on all sides and then place them on paper towels to drain the excess oil. Continue until all of the meatballs are browned. Set aside.

Over medium heat, sauté the onion in olive oil for 2–3 minutes.

Add the red pepper and mushrooms and sauté another 2–3 minutes.

Add the garlic and cook 30 seconds.

Add the tomatoes, zucchini, water, granulated sugar and seasonings, and after mixing, gently place the meatballs on top. Cover and bring the soup to a low simmer and cook 25 minutes.

Add the remaining reserved rice and lemon juice and heat through.

PER SERVING

322	Calories
19 g	Fat (54.2% calories from fat)
16 g	Protein
21 g	Carbohydrate
3 g	Dietary Fiber
70 mg	Cholesterol
711 mg	Sodium

SERVES 12 | MEAT · FREEZES

Mexican Beef Soup

¾ lb. | 375 g stewing beef, cut into ½-inch | 1-cm cubes

3 Tbsp. | 45 mL olive oil

1 small yellow onion, finely chopped

1 Tbsp. | 15 mL ground cumin

1 tsp. | 5 mL ground coriander

1–2 cloves garlic (1 tsp. | 5 mL), crushed

2½ tsp. | 12 mL salt

½ tsp. | 2 mL black pepper

1 tsp. | 5 mL chili powder

6 cups | 1.5 L cold water

1 can (16 oz. or 19 oz. | 540 mL) black beans, rinsed and drained

¾ cup | 175 mL frozen corn kernels

2 Tbsp. | 25 mL fresh lime juice

1 Tbsp. | 15 mL cilantro, chopped

¾ tsp. | 4 mL hot sauce

Serve this soup with some extra lime wedges and hot sauce so everybody can add more to suit their tastes. For a different kind of kick, throw in a chopped jalapeno with the other spices.

METHOD

In a soup pot, sauté the beef in olive oil over medium heat for 2–3 minutes, until it has been seared and is starting to brown.

Add the onion and sauté another 5–6 minutes, until it starts to brown.

Add all of the spices and cook for one minute, stirring constantly.

Add water, cover, turn the heat up to high and bring to a boil. Then reduce heat and simmer the soup on low for 45 minutes, until the meat is very tender.

Add black beans and frozen corn and cook another 5 minutes, until they are heated through.

Add lime juice, cilantro and hot sauce just before serving.

PER SERVING

250	Calories
12 g	Fat (43.4% calories from fat)
16 g	Protein
19 g	Carbohydrate
6 g	Dietary Fiber
26 mg	Cholesterol
1223 mg	Sodium

SERVES 6 | MEAT · FREEZES

Lamb and Fruit Soup

1 small yellow onion, finely chopped

3 Tbsp. | 45 mL olive oil

½ lb. | 250 g lamb shoulder, cut into ½-inch | 1-cm cubes

½ tsp. | 2 mL ground cinnamon

½ tsp. | 2 mL ground nutmeg

½ tsp. | 2 mL ground cloves

½ tsp. | 2 mL ground allspice

1 Tbsp. | 15 mL fresh ginger, finely minced

1½ tsp. | 7 mL salt

¼ tsp. | 1 mL black pepper

7 cups | 1.75 L cold water

⅔ cup | 150 mL dried apricots, cut into ¼-inch | 5-mm cubes

⅔ cup | 150 mL prunes, cut into ¼-inch | 5-mm cubes

⅔ cup | 150 mL seedless raisins

¼ cup | 50 mL pine nuts, toasted

The combination of lamb and dried fruit makes this an incredibly rich soup. The spices add beautiful aromas and flavors.

METHOD

Over medium-low heat, sauté the onion in olive oil for 7–10 minutes, until it starts to brown.

Add the lamb and continue to sauté for another 4–5 minutes, until the meat is lightly browned.

Add all the spices and cook another minute, stirring constantly.

Add the water, cover the pot and turn the heat up, bringing the soup to a boil. Reduce the heat and simmer on low for 40 minutes.

Add the dried fruit and simmer another 15 minutes, until it softens and starts to dissolve into the soup.

Garnish with the toasted pine nuts and serve.

PER SERVING

329	Calories
16 g	Fat (42.2% calories from fat)
8 g	Protein
42 g	Carbohydrate
5 g	Dietary Fiber
21 mg	Cholesterol
566 mg	Sodium

SERVES 6 | MEAT · FREEZES

Lamb and Lentil Soup

½ lb. | 250 g lamb shoulder, cut into ½-inch | 1-cm cubes

3 Tbsp. | 45 mL olive oil

2 tsp. | 10 mL ground coriander

1 Tbsp. | 15 mL ground cumin

1 tsp. | 5 mL salt

¼ tsp. | 1 mL black pepper

4–6 cloves garlic (1 Tbsp. | 15 mL), crushed

1½ cups | 375 mL dry red wine

1 can (16 oz. or 19 oz. | 540 mL) diced tomatoes

5 cups | 1.25 L water

1 small yellow onion, finely chopped

1 stalk celery, chopped into small cubes

1 large carrot, peeled and chopped into small cubes

⅔ cup | 150 mL green lentils, picked through and rinsed well

Served with some couscous, this makes a perfect Middle Eastern dinner.

METHOD

Over medium heat, in a heavy soup pot, sauté the lamb for 4–5 minutes, until lightly browned.

Add all of the seasonings and sauté another minute, stirring constantly.

Pour in the wine, tomatoes and water. Cover, turn the heat up and bring to a boil. Reduce the heat and simmer for 20 minutes on medium-low.

Add the vegetables and lentils and simmer another 35 minutes, or until the lentils are tender.

PER SERVING

231	Calories
10 g	Fat (45.0% calories from fat)
10 g	Protein
19 g	Carbohydrate
7 g	Dietary Fiber
16 mg	Cholesterol
431 mg	Sodium

SERVES 8 | MEAT • FREEZES

Fruit and Dessert Soups

Apple Soup

1½ cups | 375 mL white Zinfandel

5–6 medium Golden Delicious apples (1½ lbs. | 750 g), peeled, cored and sliced

2 medium Granny Smith apples (½ lb. | 250 g), peeled, cored and sliced

5 cups | 1.25 L stock

2 Tbsp. | 25 mL granulated sugar

¼ tsp. | 1 mL cloves, ground

¼ tsp. | 1 mL salt

¼ tsp. | 1 mL ground cinnamon

Fresh, finely chopped apples can be used for a great garnish. The contrast in textures and temperatures between the hot, puréed soup and the cool, crisp apple garnish is amazing.

METHOD

Over high heat, bring the wine to a simmer. Add the rest of the ingredients and simmer for 15 minutes, or until the apples are soft.

Purée the soup. See *Puréeing Soups* on page 9 in the Techniques section.

If you cooled the soup before puréeing, warm it through again before serving.

PER SERVING

96	Calories
1 g	Fat (10.5% calories from fat)
2 g	Protein
21 g	Carbohydrate
3 g	Dietary Fiber
0 mg	Cholesterol
1330 mg	Sodium

SERVES 6 | PARVE • FREEZES • PASSOVER

Blueberry Soup

2 lbs. | 1 kg fresh blueberries, picked through and well rinsed

1½ tsp. | 7 mL fresh rosemary, finely minced

5 cups | 1.25 L water

5 Tbsp. | 70 mL granulated sugar

¼ tsp. | 1 mL salt

⅓ cup | 75 mL sour cream

I love blueberries. When I was a kid, my family had a cottage in Ontario with wild blueberries growing in the yard. I've loved them ever since. While this soup would be amazing with wild blueberries, it's also great with cultivated berries. You could even use frozen, whole berries if fresh ones aren't available.

You don't get a strong rosemary taste in the soup, but it does add a certain je ne sais quoi.

METHOD

Place everything but the sour cream in a pot. Cover and bring to a boil over high heat. Reduce heat and simmer for 3–5 minutes, until the blueberries are soft and have started to split.

Purée the soup. See *Puréeing Soups* on page 9 in the Techniques section.

After the soup is puréed, pour through a fine-mesh strainer and use a wooden spoon to work as much liquid and flesh through, while leaving the skin and rosemary behind.

Place the soup in the refrigerator for a minimum of 4 hours. It should be well chilled before serving.

Top each bowl of chilled soup with a heaping teaspoon (5 mL) of sour cream, or if you prefer, you can substitute yogurt.

PER SERVING

114	Calories
2 g	Fat (17.8% calories from fat)
1 g	Protein
24 g	Carbohydrate
3 g	Dietary Fiber
4 mg	Cholesterol
83 mg	Sodium

SERVES 8 | DAIRY · DON'T FREEZE

Green Grape Soup

1½ lbs. | 750 g seedless green grapes

⅛ tsp. | .5 mL ground nutmeg

¼ tsp. | 1 mL ground allspice

2 cups | 500 mL water

4 Tbsp. | 60 mL granulated sugar

1 cup | 250 mL dry white wine

Serve this soup for a light starter or between dinner courses. It's elegant and refreshing.

METHOD

Put all the ingredients into a soup pot, cover and place over high heat. Bring soup to a boil. Reduce heat and simmer for 5 minutes, or until the grape skins start to split.

Purée the soup. See *Puréeing Soups* on page 9 in the Techniques section.

Pour the soup through a fine-mesh strainer to remove any seeds and skin and transfer into a clean bowl. Chill the soup for a minimum of 4 hours, or until the soup is completely cold.

PER SERVING

126	Calories
trace	Fat (1.5% calories from fat)
1 g	Protein
24 g	Carbohydrate
1 g	Dietary Fiber
0 mg	Cholesterol
14 mg	Sodium

SERVES 5 | PARVE • DON'T FREEZE • PASSOVER

Melon Gazpacho

1 small honeydew melon, peeled and seeded

1 small cantaloupe, peeled and seeded

1 small red onion, peeled

1 small red pepper, cored and seeded

1 large English (long seedless) cucumber, peeled and seeded

1–2 cloves garlic (1 tsp. | 5 mL), crushed

2 Tbsp. | 25 mL olive oil

2 Tbsp. | 25 mL fresh lemon juice

2 Tbsp. | 25 mL fresh lime juice

2 tsp. | 10 mL salt

¼ tsp. | 1 mL black pepper

2 Tbsp. | 25 mL fresh chives, finely chopped

2 Tbsp. | 25 mL fresh parsley, finely chopped

2 Tbsp. | 25 mL fresh mint, finely chopped

A refreshing twist on gazpacho. Use only really ripe melons. Perfect for summer lunches.

METHOD

Reserve a third of the honeydew melon and cantaloupe. Cut this reserved melon into small dice.

In a food processor or blender, purée red onion, red pepper, cucumber, garlic, olive oil, lemon juice, lime juice and the remaining two-thirds of the melon. If you need to, purée the soup in batches.

Transfer puréed mixture into a bowl and stir in salt, pepper, fresh herbs and diced melon. Or reserve the diced melon to be used as a garnish for the soup when it is served. Chill for a minimum of 4 hours. Best if left to chill overnight.

PER SERVING

102	Calories
6 g	Fat (46.9% calories from fat)
2 g	Protein
13 g	Carbohydrate
2 g	Dietary Fiber
0 mg	Cholesterol
863 mg	Sodium

SERVES 5 | PARVE · DON'T FREEZE · PASSOVER

Orange Gazpacho

2 medium mangos, peeled, cut away from the stone

1 small cantaloupe, peeled, seeded and coarsely chopped

1 medium orange bell pepper, cored and seeded

1 medium English (long seedless) cucumber, peeled, seeded and cut into large chunks

3 oranges, peeled, seeded and sectioned

½ cup | 125 mL fresh basil leaves, lightly packed

1 small shallot, peeled and coarsely chopped

1 tsp. | 5 mL salt

1 Tbsp. | 15 mL balsamic vinegar

1 Tbsp. | 15 mL olive oil

¼ tsp. | 1 mL black pepper

There is a huge debate concerning smooth versus chunky. I like the base of gazpacho to be as smooth as possible, with a fine dice of the main flavors added for texture. Some folks like to purée everything until they get the smoothest of soups, chunk free. Others prefer to only pulse the food processor and create a totally chunky soup. Try it all three ways to see which one you prefer.

METHOD

Reserve a third of the mango, cantaloupe and orange pepper, and chop into fine dice, ⅛-inch (3-mm) to ¼-inch (5-mm) cubes.

Place the rest of the ingredients in a food processor or blender and purée until very smooth. If your food processor doesn't have a large enough capacity, process in batches.

Stir in the reserved diced fruit and refrigerate a minimum of 4 hours. It's even better when you prepare it a day before and let all of the flavors mingle overnight. If you prefer, the reserved fruit can be left out and used as a garnish when the soup is served.

PER SERVING

87	Calories
3 g	Fat (24.4% calories from fat)
1 g	Protein
16 g	Carbohydrate
3 g	Dietary Fiber
0 mg	Cholesterol
361 mg	Sodium

SERVES 6 | PARVE · DON'T FREEZE · PASSOVER

Pear Soup with Feta, Pecans and Balsamic Reduction

1 cup | 250 mL balsamic vinegar

5–6 medium Bosc pears (2 lbs. | 1 kg), peeled, cored and cubed

2 cups | 500 mL stock

½ tsp. | 2 mL salt

⅛ tsp. | .5 mL black pepper

⅓ cup | 75 mL feta cheese, crumbled

½ cup | 125 mL toasted pecans, chopped

This soup works best as a starter—half-cup (125-mL) portions are all you need. The reduced balsamic, feta and pecans add amazing texture and flavor. I like to serve the soup with the vinegar reduction drizzled on top, garnished with the feta and pecans. This way your guests can mix it together or have something different in each spoon!

METHOD

For the balsamic reduction, bring the vinegar to a boil, then reduce the heat to very low and simmer gently for approximately 20 minutes. The vinegar should reduce to ⅓ cup (75 mL) and will thicken and become syrupy. Set the reduction aside.

Place the pears, stock, salt and pepper in a pot and bring to a boil over high heat. Reduce the heat and simmer for 12–15 minutes, until the pears are fork-tender.

Purée the soup. See *Puréeing Soups* on page 9 in the Techniques section.

Garnish with balsamic reduction, crumbled feta and chopped, toasted pecans.

PER SERVING

137	Calories
7 g	Fat (40.6% calories from fat)
2 g	Protein
20 g	Carbohydrate
3 g	Dietary Fiber
6 mg	Cholesterol
584 mg	Sodium

SERVES 8 | DAIRY · DON'T FREEZE

❧ Red Grape Soup

1½ lbs. | 750 g seedless red grapes

⅛ tsp. | .5 mL ground cloves

¼ tsp. | 1 mL ground allspice

2 cups | 500 mL water

¼ cup | 50 mL granulated sugar

1 cup | 250 mL dry red wine

This lovely, elegant chilled soup is wonderful as a starter. Taste one of the grapes before you cook them; if they are exceptionally sweet, you may want to hold off on adding the granulated sugar.

METHOD

Place all the ingredients into a soup pot, cover and bring to a boil over high heat. Reduce heat and simmer on low for 5 minutes, or until the grape skins start to split.

Purée the soup. See *Puréeing Soups* on page 9 in the Techniques section.

Pour the soup through a fine-mesh strainer to remove any seeds and skin and transfer into a clean bowl. Chill the soup for a minimum of 4 hours, or until the soup is completely cold.

PER SERVING

128	Calories
trace	Fat (1.4% calories from fat)
1 g	Protein
25 g	Carbohydrate
1 g	Dietary Fiber
0 mg	Cholesterol
42 mg	Sodium

SERVES 5 | PARVE • DON'T FREEZE • PASSOVER

Strawberry Sambuca Soup

3 lbs. | 1.5 kg strawberries, hulled and sliced into ¼-inch | 5-mm slices

4 oz. | 125 g granulated sugar

1 cup | 250 mL water

½ tsp. | 2 mL black pepper

3 Tbsp. | 45 mL sambuca or anisette

When I first tasted strawberries and black pepper, I was shocked at how well they went together. The sambuca adds just a touch of liquorice flavor and works amazingly well with the strawberries. Before adding the granulated sugar, taste a strawberry. If they are exceptionally sweet, you may want to hold back some of the granulated sugar; if they are slightly underripe, add a little extra.

METHOD

Place the strawberries, granulated sugar, water and black pepper in a covered soup pot over high heat and bring to a boil. Reduce the temperature and simmer for 5 minutes, or until the strawberries have softened.

Purée the soup. See *Puréeing Soups* on page 9 in the Techniques section.

Pour the puréed soup through a fine-mesh strainer to remove any seeds or chunks.

Add the sambuca or anisette and chill for a minimum of 4 hours, or until the soup has completely chilled.

PER SERVING

157	Calories
1 g	Fat (4.3% calories from fat)
1 g	Protein
34 g	Carbohydrate
5 g	Dietary Fiber
0 mg	Cholesterol
4 mg	Sodium

SERVES 6 | PARVE · DON'T FREEZE

Strawberry Soup

2 lbs. | 1 kg strawberries, stems removed, cleaned and sliced

1 cup | 250 mL white Zinfandel

6 Tbsp. | 90 mL granulated sugar

1 cup | 250 mL water

¼ cup | 50 mL creamy style non-fat yogurt

2 Tbsp. | 25 mL fresh lemon juice

½ cup | 125 mL half-and-half

This is a light and refreshing soup. Make it during the summer when strawberries are at their best and a cool soup is most enjoyable.

METHOD

Place the cleaned and sliced strawberries in a bowl with the wine and granulated sugar, mix well and set aside for about an hour and a half.

Pour the strawberry mixture and water into a saucepan, cover and bring to a boil over high heat. Turn the heat down and simmer gently for 5–7 minutes.

Take the soup off the heat and pour through a fine-mesh colander. Using a metal spoon, gently push the strawberry flesh through the strainer. Discard any seeds and fibrous particles that won't go through the mesh.

Chill the soup for at least 4 hours. You can actually leave the soup at this point, covered, overnight in the refrigerator.

Before serving, combine the strawberry mixture with the yogurt, lemon juice and half-and-half.

PER SERVING

124	Calories
3 g	Fat (19.2% calories from fat)
2 g	Protein
25 g	Carbohydrate
3 g	Dietary Fiber
8 mg	Cholesterol
19 mg	Sodium

SERVES 6 | DAIRY • FREEZES

Chocolate Soup

6 Tbsp. | 90 mL granulated sugar

3 egg yolks

2 cups | 500 mL half-and-half

2 cups | 500 mL 2% milk

pinch salt

2 cups | 500 mL semi-sweet chocolate chips
(12 oz. | 375 g)

3 Tbsp. | 45 mL unsweetened cocoa powder

This creamy soup makes a great dessert. Serve it with a little fresh-whipped cream and some sliced strawberries or use it as a cold chocolate fondue. Guests will be surprised when you serve this one!

METHOD

In a mixing bowl, whisk together the granulated sugar and the egg yolks until frothy and butter colored.

Using a double-boiler (or place about 2 inches / 5 cm of water in a saucepan, bring to a light simmer and place a metal bowl over it), heat the half-and-half, milk, salt, chocolate and cocoa powder until all of the chocolate is melted and the mixture has warmed through.

Slowly add some of the hot chocolate mixture, about ½ cup (125 mL), into the egg/granulated sugar mixture, whisking as you pour it, so that the hot liquid is incorporated right away and the eggs don't scramble. Slowly pour this mixture back into the hot chocolate, whisking as you pour. Continue to heat the soup until it has thickened slightly, 3–5 minutes, whisking continuously. When you dip a wooden spoon into the soup, then drag a fingertip through the coating on the spoon, the line where you've dragged your finger should remain clean.

Transfer the soup to a bowl or container, cover with wax paper and refrigerate at least 4 hours, or until the soup is completely chilled.

PER SERVING

376	Calories
23 g	Fat (50.9% calories from fat)
7 g	Protein
43 g	Carbohydrate
3 g	Dietary Fiber
107 mg	Cholesterol
63 mg	Sodium

SERVES 8 | DAIRY · DON'T FREEZE · PASSOVER · DESSERT

Accompaniments

Croutons

1 lb. | 500 g loaf French bread, cut into
¾-inch | 2-cm cubes

¼ cup | 50 mL butter or margarine

2–4 cloves garlic (2 tsp. | 10 mL), crushed

Croutons make a great garnish for soups. French Onion Soup (see page 24) with garlic croutons and Parmesan cheese makes a great lunch. You can freeze the croutons in plastic bags and allow them to thaw on a baking sheet when you want to use them.

For different flavors, try adding ½ to 1 tsp. (2 to 5 mL) of your favorite dried herbs to the butter or margarine. My favorite is oregano.

METHOD

Preheat the oven to 325°F (160°C). Place bread cubes in a mixing bowl. Melt the butter or margarine in a microwave-safe bowl, or in a pot on the stovetop, and mix in the crushed garlic. Pour the garlic butter over the bread cubes and toss well.

Place the bread in a single layer on baking trays lined with parchment paper and bake for 20–25 minutes, until the croutons are toasty brown and crunchy. Turn the croutons over halfway through baking so they cook evenly on both sides.

PER SERVING

104	Calories
4 g	Fat (32.3% calories from fat)
3 g	Protein
15 g	Carbohydrate
1 g	Dietary Fiber
0 mg	Cholesterol
206 mg	Sodium

SERVES 16 | PARVE/DAIRY · FREEZES

❧ Dumplings

2 eggs

¼ cup | 50 mL water

½ tsp. | 2 mL salt

½ tsp. | 2 mL black pepper

1 cup | 250 mL all-purpose flour

(water or stock for cooking)

These dumplings are perfect for the Creamy Chicken Rice Soup (without the rice), page 117, but try them with any soup you like!

METHOD

In a small bowl, whisk together the eggs, water, salt and pepper with a fork. Add the flour and mix well.

Using 2 spoons, drop small amounts (about 1 tsp. | 5 mL) into gently simmering water or soup. Cover and simmer for about 10 minutes. The dumplings are done when you cut into one and it is cooked through.

PER SERVING

98	Calories
2 g	Fat (15.7% calories from fat)
4 g	Protein
16 g	Carbohydrate
1 g	Dietary Fiber
62 mg	Cholesterol
197 mg	Sodium

SERVES 6 | PARVE · DON'T FREEZE

❧ Egg Noodles

2 cups | 500 mL all-purpose flour

2 Tbsp. | 25 mL water

1 Tbsp. | 15 mL olive oil

2 large eggs

(water or stock for cooking)

These are perfect for homemade chicken noodle soup. I like them rolled out and cut as thin as possible. But because you make them yourself, you can make them any shape you want!

METHOD

Place the flour in a mixing bowl and form a well in the center. Pour the water, oil and eggs into the well. Using a fork, start to mix all of the liquid together, slowly bringing more and more flour in from the sides as you go. Eventually you want to incorporate all of the flour.

Turn the mixture out onto a lightly floured work table and start kneading. Knead the dough for about 10 minutes, or until it is smooth and elastic.

Shape the dough into a disk and wrap it in plastic wrap. Refrigerate for at least 1 hour, and allow the dough to relax.

Slice the dough into smaller pieces and use a pasta machine or rolling pin to roll it out as thin as you like. I like to roll it from $\frac{1}{8}$ inch to $\frac{1}{16}$ inch (1.5 to 3mm) thick. Slice the noodles into whatever width you like.

Allow the noodles to dry a little on a cookie sheet as you bring the water or stock to a boil. Add the noodles and simmer for 5–10 minutes, depending on their thickness. The best way to test is to bite into one. Don't walk away and forget about the noodles, because they will overcook easily. The thinner they are, the less time they need to cook.

PER SERVING

116	Calories
2 g	Fat (19.6% calories from fat)
4 g	Protein
19 g	Carbohydrate
1 g	Dietary Fiber
37 mg	Cholesterol
12 mg	Sodium

SERVES 10 | PARVE • FREEZES

Blueberry Soup | *page 147*

Melon Gazpacho | *page 149*

Chocolate Soup | *page 155*

Pear Soup with Feta, Pecans and Balsamic Reduction | *page 151*

Matzo Balls

3 eggs

¼ cup | 50 mL water

2 Tbsp. | 25 mL olive oil

1¼ tsp. | 6 mL salt

¼ tsp. | 1 mL black pepper

½ tsp. | 2 mL garlic powder

½ tsp. | 2 mL onion powder

1 cup | 250 mL matzo meal

(water or stock for cooking)

Homemade chicken soup and matzo balls are perfect partners. The debate is hard versus light and fluffy. I prefer them on the fluffy side. This recipe compromises and produces a matzo ball that's not too hard and not too fluffy. Just perfect.

METHOD

In a bowl, whisk the eggs, water, olive oil, salt, pepper, garlic powder and onion powder together with a fork. Add the matzo meal and mix well. Cover with plastic wrap and refrigerate for at least 20 minutes, giving the matzo meal a chance to absorb the liquids.

Form the mixture into 14–18 walnut-sized balls. You may need to dip your hands into cold water to keep the mixture from sticking to them.

Carefully place the matzo balls into gently simmering water or stock. Cover and simmer for 30–45 minutes. They are ready when you cut into one and it is cooked all the way through.

PER SERVING

121	Calories
5 g	Fat (40.3% calories from fat)
4 g	Protein
14 g	Carbohydrate
1 g	Dietary Fiber
70 mg	Cholesterol
355 mg	Sodium

SERVES 8 | PARVE · FREEZES · PASSOVER

Matzo Balls with Fresh Herbs

3 eggs

¼ cup | 50 mL water

2 Tbsp. | 25 mL olive oil

1¼ tsp. | 6 mL salt

¼ tsp. | 1 mL black pepper

½ tsp . | 2 mL garlic powder

½ tsp. | 2 mL onion powder

1 Tbsp. | 15 mL fresh dill, finely chopped

1 Tbsp. | 15 mL fresh parsley, finely chopped

1 cup | 250 mL matzo meal

(water or stock for cooking)

A dressed-up version of the matzo ball.

METHOD

In a bowl, whisk the eggs, water, olive oil, salt, pepper, garlic powder, onion powder, dill and parsley together with a fork. Add the matzo meal and mix well. Cover with plastic wrap and refrigerate for at least 20 minutes, giving the matzo meal a chance to absorb the liquids.

Form the mixture into 14–18 walnut-sized balls. You may need to dip your hands into cold water to keep the mixture from sticking to them.

Carefully place the matzo balls into gently simmering water or stock. Cover and simmer for 30–45 minutes. They are ready when you cut into one and it is cooked all the way through.

PER SERVING

121	Calories
5 g	Fat (40.2% calories from fat)
4 g	Protein
14 g	Carbohydrate
1 g	Dietary Fiber
70 mg	Cholesterol
355 mg	Sodium

SERVES 8 | PARVE · FREEZES · PASSOVER

Index